"With the heart of a pastor and the skill of an a
refreshing insight into the practical as well as th
justification. It's essential reading at a time when
ing attack."

MICHAEL S. HORTON
Associate Professor of Historical Theology and Apologetics
Westminster Theological Seminary in California

"I share the concern of John Piper as he not only sounds the alarm but also rushes to
the rescue of all who are tempted to abandon a truly biblical perspective on the issue of
imputation."

ALISTAIR BEGG
Senior Pastor, Parkside Church, Cleveland

"Although I have been a Christian for a long time, I became aware of the doctrine of
the imputation of Christ's active righteousness only fairly recently. Yet in the years since
I have become aware of the 'Blessed Exchange'—my sin for Christ's righteousness—I
doubt that a day has gone by without my feasting on this core truth of biblical faith.
Consequently, I am deeply grateful to John Piper for his careful articulation and defense
of this, the 'leading edge' of Christianity's Good News. Piper also shows how our faithfully embracing this liberating truth should radically affect our daily Christian lives. As
Augustine heard the child chant, 'Take and read.'"

MARK R. TALBOT
Associate Professor of Philosophy
Wheaton College
Executive Editor, *Modern Reformation* magazine

"This is a superb work, wonderful in its clarity, remarkable for its faithful, thorough
treatment of the biblical texts, and powerful in the force of its argument. Dr. Piper's sim-
ple, potent answer to the recent attacks on the historic Protestant understanding of justification by faith will cure a host of theological ills. This is surely one of the finest and
most important books to be published in many years."

JOHN MACARTHUR
Pastor, Grace Community Church, Sun Valley, California
President, The Master's College

"John Piper's book on Christ's imputed righteousness is exactly what the current debate
over this issue needs. Dr. Piper demonstrates through a precise and persuasive exegesis
of the relevant passages that this doctrine is both biblical and important. He argues pas-
sionately that understanding the doctrine is spiritually edifying and pastorally helpful.
He does all this, moreover, in a charitable, irenic tone suitable for a teaching that is such
good news."

FRANK THIELMAN
Presbyterian Professor of Divinity
Beeson Divinity School, Samford University

"Now I know something of the shock Augustine must have felt when he initially read
Pelagius. My heart is pained that the cardinal doctrine of the Christian faith is called
nonsense and passé by friends. Without imputed righteousness Christianity is not
Christian, divine justice is made a folly, and sin is requited by mere human sincerity. It
is too much to surrender the wonderfully comforting, biblically clear truth that we stand
before a holy God clothed and complete in the righteousness of His Son. I thank God
that someone has spoken out!"

JOHN D. HANNAH
Department Chairman, Distinguished Professor of Historical Theology
Dallas Theological Seminary

"With a mind deeply saturated in God's word, a heart longing for the church's purity and confidence, and a passion that Christ be honored in all and above all, John Piper writes *Counted Righteous in Christ* to guide a new generation of Christians into the glorious truth of our justification by faith alone, in Christ alone. One cannot help but marvel at and rejoice in the care with which Piper treats relevant passages. Often countering popular and novel proposals, he gives clear and compelling reasons for seeing justification as, centrally, the crediting of Christ's very own and perfect righteousness to the one who trusts in God alone for his salvation. No doctrine is more basic to God's salvation plan and hence more central in understanding the Christian's new identity; yet today these truths are widely ignored or misunderstood. Believer, I commend you to read this book with justified hopes of entering more fully into the liberating freedom of your full and certain righteous standing before the God who justifies the ungodly (marvel!) through faith in the merits of his Son's righteous life and substitutionary death."

BRUCE A. WARE
Senior Associate Dean, School of Theology
Professor of Theology
The Southern Baptist Theological Seminary

"This is a timely and important work. Four times in the past four days I have been shocked to read of well-known evangelicals challenging some aspect of the historic, Reformation view of justification. As an eroding tide of evangelical opinion rises against it, may the Lord use John's book to reinforce the theological retaining wall around the lighthouse doctrine of justification."

DON WHITNEY
Associate Professor of Spiritual Formation
Midwestern Baptist Theological Seminary

"The unraveling of evangelical commitment seems always to have a new chapter. In *Counted Righteous in Christ*, Dr. John Piper has isolated the newest retreat on the doctrine of the imputed righteousness of Christ. This book restates in powerful terms the necessity of Christ's righteousness becoming our own."

PAIGE PATTERSON
President, Professor of Theology
Southeastern Theological Baptist Seminary

"Dr. Piper writes not only with his customary verve and enthusiasm but also with the courtesy and charity we have come to expect of him, as he robustly defends the traditional doctrine of the imputation of Christ's righteousness. Those who think that this teaching is neither biblical nor essential to the Christian faith, and can therefore be quietly dropped, will need to weigh Dr. Piper's arguments carefully, particularly his exposition of the Pauline teaching on righteousness and justification."

PETER T. O'BRIEN
Senior Research Fellow in New Testament and Vice Principal
Moore Theological College, Sydney, Australia

"Piper provides a passionate, well-informed, and convincing exposition of the centrality of the imputed righteousness of Christ for the justification of sinners. In response to a growing number of scholars and church leaders who have questioned the traditional Protestant understanding of justification, Piper offers a lucid and compelling examination of the biblical evidence in support of that understanding. His many fresh insights and practical applications will challenge the complacent, comfort the afflicted, and inspire lives of grateful praise on the part of those who are the beneficiaries of Christ's redeeming work."

THE REV. GORDON P. HUGENBERGER
Senior Minister, Park Street Church, Boston
Adjunct Professor of Old Testament, Gordon-Conwell Theological Seminary

"Largely a result of the emergence in recent decades of the 'new perspective' on Paul is the growing denial today that the apostle teaches the imputation of Christ's righteousness to believers. *Counted Righteous in Christ* is such an important book because it confronts this denial head-on and counters the charge that the heart of the Reformation doctrine of justification rests on a misunderstanding of Scripture. Written in the author's typically spirited and winsome fashion, it provides what is most urgently needed in the face of this charge: a clear and convincing *exegetical* case for the gospel truth affirmed in its title. The broader church is deeply indebted to John Piper for what it has been given to him to produce in the midst of the already overly full demands of a busy pastorate."

> RICHARD B. GAFFIN, JR.
> Professor of Biblical and Systematic Theology
> Westminster Theological Seminary, Philadelphia

"John Piper's defense of the Reformation's traditional interpretation of the imputation of Christ's righteousness deserves to be taken very seriously. Expert biblical scholars must, in the end, judge the details of his exegesis, but all careful readers should be able to see that he has presented a telling account of the practical spiritual value of the doctrine, its centrality in the church's most enduring hymnody, and its critical importance in the theology of the New Testament."

> MARK A. NOLL
> McManis Chair of Christian Thought
> Wheaton College

"In this exegetical study John Piper carefully demonstrates the importance and the biblical basis of the doctrine of imputation of Christ's righteousness to the believer. This is important reading in light of recent challenges to the traditional understanding of justification."

> MILLARD J. ERICKSON
> Distinguished Professor of Theology
> Truett Seminary, Baylor University

"While the biblical doctrine of justification is about more than imputation, it does not involve less. John Piper has written a vigorous and timely book on this neglected and yet critically important theme. From the historic Protestant perspective, the doctrine of imputation underscores the radical character of divine grace, and John makes this point with clarity, passion, and insight."

> TIMOTHY GEORGE
> Dean, Beeson Divinity School, Samford University
> Executive Editor, *Christianity Today*

"While evangelicals sleep, people we once trusted have been sowing seeds of false doctrine in the church. Responding to the latest departure from the faith, John Piper challenges those who have abandoned the pivotal doctrine of the imputation of Christ's righteousness. What is at stake here is nothing less than the integrity of the Gospel."

> RONALD H. NASH
> Professor of Philosophy
> The Southern Baptist Theological Seminary

Counted Righteous in Christ

OTHER BOOKS BY JOHN PIPER

Desiring God: Meditations of a Christian Hedonist

The Dangerous Duty of Delight: The Glorified God and the Satisfied Soul

The Pleasures of God: Meditations on God's Delight in Being God

The Purifying Power of Living by Faith in FUTURE GRACE

God's Passion for His Glory: Living the Vision of Jonathan Edwards

A Hunger for God: Desiring God Through Prayer and Fasting

Let the Nations Be Glad! The Supremacy of God in Missions,
Revised and Expanded

The Supremacy of God in Preaching

Brothers, We Are Not Professionals: A Plea to Pastors for Radical Ministry

Recovering Biblical Manhood and Womanhood:
A Response to Evangelical Feminism (co-edited with Wayne Grudem)

What's the Difference? Manhood and Womanhood
Defined According to the Bible

A Godward Life: Savoring the Supremacy of God in All of Life

A Godward Life, Book Two: Savoring the Supremacy of God in All of Life

The Justification of God:
An Exegetical and Theological Study of Romans 9:1-23

The Innkeeper

The Misery of Job and the Mercy of God
(with photography by Ric Ergenbright)

The Legacy of Sovereign Joy: God's Triumphant Grace in the Lives of
Augustine, Luther, and Calvin

The Hidden Smile of God: The Fruit of Affliction in the Lives of
John Bunyan, William Cowper, and David Brainerd

The Roots of Endurance: Invincible Perseverance in the Lives of
John Newton, Charles Simeon, and William Wilberforce

Seeing and Savoring Jesus Christ

Beyond the Bounds: Open Theism & the Undermining of
Biblical Christianity (co-edited with Justin Taylor & Paul Kjoss Helseth)

Dear Donna,
you are loved,
Dad^2 and Mom^2
Nov 16, 2016

COUNTED
RIGHTEOUS
IN
CHRIST

Should We Abandon the Imputation of
Christ's Righteousness?

JOHN PIPER

CROSSWAY BOOKS

A DIVISION OF
GOOD NEWS PUBLISHERS
WHEATON, ILLINOIS

Cover design: Liita Forsyth

First printing, 2002

Printed in the United States of America

Unless otherwise indicated, all Scripture quotations are the author's own translation.

Also quoted in this book:

The Holy Bible, English Standard Version (ESV), copyright © 2001 by Crossway Bibles, a division of Good News Publishers. Used by permission. All rights reserved

New American Standard Bible (NASB) copyright © 1960, 1962, 1963, 1968, 1971, 1972, 1973, 1975, 1977, 1995 by the Lockman Foundation. Used by permission.

Library of Congress Cataloging-in-Publication Data
Piper, John, 1946-
  Counted righteous in Christ : should we abandon the imputation of Christ's righteousness? / John Piper.
    p. cm.
  Includes index.
  ISBN 1-58134-447-3 (tpb : alk. paper)
    1. Justification—Biblical teaching. 2. Bible. N.T. Epistles of Paul—Criticism, interpretation, etc. I. Title.
BS2655.J8 P54   2002
234'.7—dc21   2002009041

DP		13	12	11	10	09	08	07	06	05	04	03	02
15	14	13	12	11	10	9	8	7	6	5	4	3	2	1

To
MATT PERMAN
DUSTIN SHRAMEK
GARY STEWARD
JUSTIN TAYLOR
TODD WILSON
STEPHEN WITMER

The first class of
THE BETHLEHEM INSTITUTE
without whose careful biblical queries
this book would not exist

CONTENTS

PREFACE   13

FULL OUTLINE OF THE ARGUMENT   17

CHAPTER ONE
THE SETTING IN FAMILY, CHURCH, CULTURE,   21
    AND NATIONS

CHAPTER TWO
THE CONTEMPORARY CHALLENGE   41

CHAPTER THREE
AN EXEGETICAL RESPONSE TO THE CHALLENGE   53

CHAPTER FOUR
CONCLUSION   121

NOTE ON RESOURCES: DESIRING GOD MINISTRIES   126
SCRIPTURE INDEX   129
NAME INDEX   133
SUBJECT INDEX   137

PREFACE

As I have preached through the first eight chapters of Paul's letter to the Romans in the last four years, I have found my mind and heart moving toward Luther's estimation of the doctrine of justification, and particularly the imputation of Christ's righteousness as the precious foundation of our full acceptance and everlasting inheritance of life and joy.

> [Justification is] the chief article of Christian doctrine. To him who understands how great its usefulness and majesty are, everything else will seem slight and turn to nothing. For what is Peter? What is Paul? What is an angel from heaven? What are all creatures in comparison with the article of justification? For if we know this article, we are in the clearest light; if we do not know it, we dwell in the densest darkness. Therefore if you see this article impugned or imperiled, do not hesitate to resist Peter or an angel from heaven; for it cannot be sufficiently extolled.[1]

I do believe that the article is "impugned [and] imperiled" in our day. And while I would rather glory in it than argue for it, sometimes resistance is a form of rejoicing. "For everything there is a season, and a time for every matter under heaven . . . a time to break down, and a time to build up . . . a time to tear, and a time to sew; a time to keep silence, and a time to speak . . . a time

---

[1] From his exposition of Galatians 2:11 in *What Luther Says: An Anthology*, Vol. 2, ed. Ewald M. Plass (St. Louis: Concordia Publishing House, 1959), p. 705, entry 2200. Luther clarifies the nature of justification in terms of imputation of Christ's righteousness: "Christ is promised, who is your perfect and everlasting Righteousness" (p. 668, entry 2071). "If we believe in Christ, we are considered absolutely just for His sake, in faith. Later, after the death of his flesh, in the other life, we shall attain perfect righteousness and have within us the absolute righteousness which we now have only by imputation through the merit of Christ. . ."

for war, and a time for peace" (Ecclesiastes 3:1-8, ESV). A time to delight in the truth and a time to defend the truth. For the sake of delight.

Chapter One will explain why I have invested so much energy in this controversy. For now, I would simply say that the glory of Christ is the most precious reality in the universe, and it is obscured when the doctrine of justification is lost or blurred for the people of God and the mission of the church. I pray that this small effort will help preserve the "usefulness and majesty" of this truth. I offer it as a fallible act of worship in the hope that "Christ for righteousness" (Romans 10:4) will be more "sufficiently extolled."

I hope that thinking laypeople, pastors, and scholars will read this book. Chapters 1, 2, and 4 are, I believe, readable and hope-giving to the ordinary layperson. Chapter 3 is a rigorous and demanding exegetical argument. But disciplined minds can follow the argument without advanced theological training or foreign languages. In fact I would encourage the effort. Raking is easy, but all you get is leaves. Digging is hard, but you might find gold.

I have dedicated the book to the first class of The Bethlehem Institute because their questions for two years drove me back to the texts again and again to see things more clearly. I thank God for my comrade Tom Steller, whose challenges focused my energies on the crucial issues. I thank God for the Council of Elders of Bethlehem Baptist Church who freed me at least three times to do this work, because they really believe that it matters for the church and the cause of Christ in the world. And I thank God for the partnership of Lane Dennis and the team at Crossway Books for sharing the burden I have in this book.

Justin Taylor and Matt Perman deserve special thanks because of the extraordinary assistance they gave in helping conceive and assemble this final version of the book. Matt also provided the subject index, and Carol Steinbach, with her usual excellence, provided the text and person indexes. As always, my wife Noël read it all, and caught mistakes that others didn't. Finally, thanks to Robert Gundry for his perhaps unwitting assistance in bringing it all to a crisis for me, so that my thinking moved from brain to book. He graciously read my exegetical arguments against his view and allowed me to quote his correspondence. He is not persuaded. May God give us light and move all his people toward the fullest understanding and enjoyment of Christ, our righteousness.

FULL OUTLINE OF THE ARGUMENT

CHAPTER ONE:
THE SETTING IN FAMILY, CHURCH, CULTURE, AND NATIONS

CHAPTER TWO:
THE CONTEMPORARY CHALLENGE

§1. Definition and aim.
§2. Three things have moved me to write.
    §2.1. Preaching through Romans.
    §2.2. Controversy and awakenings.
    §2.3. A blast from *Books and Culture*.
§3. Summary of the challenge to historic Protestant teaching.
    §3.1. Our righteousness consists of faith.
    §3.2. There is no imputation of divine righteousness.
    §3.3. Justification has to do with liberation from sin's mastery.
    §3.4. Abandonment of the imputation of Christ as unbiblical.
§4. Defending imputation is not a rearguard action.
    §4.1 Central Reformation battles were not in vain.
    §4.2 The distinction between justification and sanctification matters.
    §4.3 The glory of Christ and the care of souls are at stake.

CHAPTER THREE:
AN EXEGETICAL RESPONSE TO THE CHALLENGE

§1. The evidence that the righteousness imputed to us is external and not our faith.
    §1.1. Paul thinks of justification in terms of "imputing" or "crediting."
    §1.2. The context of imputation is one of crediting in a book-keeping metaphor.
    §1.3. Confirmation from the connection between Romans 4:5 and 4:6.

§1.3.1. The parallel between *apart from works* in verse 6 and *the ungodly* in verse 5.

§1.3.2. The parallel between God's *justifying* in verse 5 and God's *imputing righteousness* in verse 6.

§1.4. A confirming parallel between Romans 4:6 and Romans 3:28.

§1.5. The evidence from how Paul's thought flows in Romans 4:9-11.

§1.6. Confirming evidence from Romans 10:10.

§1.7. Evidence from Philippians 3:8-9.

§1.8. A clarifying analogy for "faith imputed for righteousness."

§1.9. Conclusion: Our imputed righteousness does not consist of faith but is received by faith.

§2. The external righteousness credited to us is God's.

§2.1. The flow of thought from Romans 3:20 to 4:6.

§2.1.1. God's righteousness witnessed by the law connects with Romans 4:3.

§2.1.2. Imputed righteousness is "the righteousness of God through faith."

§2.2. The evidence for imputed divine righteousness in 2 Corinthians 5:21.

§2.3. Conclusion: God imputes his righteousness to us through faith.

§3. Justification is not liberation from sin's mastery.

§3.1. A controlling biblical-theological paradigm?

§3.2. Does the new paradigm do justice to Romans 3:24-26?

§3.3. How the new paradigm mishandles justification in Romans 6:6-7.

§3.3.1. The meaning of "justified from sin" in Romans 6:7.

§3.3.2. Another way to understand Romans 6:6-7.

§3.3.2.1. The structure of Romans: Justification is the prior basis of sanctification.

§3.3.2.2. The bondage of guilt makes justification a necessary ground for liberation.

§3.4. The flow of thought in Romans 8:3-4.

§3.5. Conclusion: Justification is not liberation from sin's mastery.

§4. **Is the divine righteousness imputed to believers the righteousness of Christ?**

§4.1. The evidence from 2 Corinthians 5:21.

§4.2. The evidence from Philippians 3:9.

§4.3. The evidence from 1 Corinthians 1:30.

§4.4. The evidence from Romans 10:4.

§4.5. The evidence from Romans 5:12-19.

§4.5.1. The incomplete sentence of Romans 5:12.

§4.5.2. The clarification of "all sinned" (verse 12) in Romans 5:13-14.

§4.5.2.1. How Paul deals with possible objections.

§4.5.2.1.1. The principle of no transgressions where there is no law.

§4.5.2.1.2. Absence of law raises the legal issue of the death sentence for all men.

§4.5.2.2. Why did Paul introduce the Adam-Christ connection at this place?

§4.5.3. The contrast between Adam and Christ in Romans 5:15-17.

§4.5.4. The crucial contrasts of Romans 5:18-19.

§4.5.5. Does Christ's "one act of righteousness" refer to his life of obedience?

§5. **The relationship between Christ's "blood and righteousness."**

§5.1. The meaning of "justify" (δικαιόω, *dikaioō*).

§5.2. Texts pointing to the imputation of righteousness.

§5.3. Justification and forgiveness in relation to the use of Psalm 32 in Romans 4.

CHAPTER FOUR:
CONCLUSION

1

THE SETTING IN FAMILY, CHURCH, CULTURE, AND NATIONS

Why would a pressured pastor with a family to care for, a flock to shepherd, weekly messages to prepare, a personal concern for wayward children, a love for biblical counseling, a burden for racial justice, a commitment to see abortion become unthinkable, a zeal for world evangelization, a focus on local church planting, and a life-goal of spreading a passion for the supremacy of God in all things for the joy of all peoples through Jesus Christ devote so much time and energy to the controversy over the imputation of Christ's righteousness?[1] And why should schoolteachers, engineers, accountants, firemen, computer programmers, and homemakers take the time to work through a book like this?

MY LIMITS

I will try to answer that question in this chapter. My answer moves from the general to the specific. That is, from reasons for caring about doctrine to reasons for caring about justification by faith to reasons for caring about the imputation of the righteousness of Christ. Implicit in my question is a disclaimer. I do not

---

[1] For a definition of these terms see Chapter Two, §1.

have the time or the heart to read as widely as scholars in academia do and should. So my focus is limited[2]—but, I hope, not shallow or exegetically flimsy. A fuller treatment of the breadth and variety of issues surrounding the doctrine of justification today can be found in many places.[3] With that said, I ask again, Why does a pastor—or why should you—take up a complex doctrinal controversy on the imputation of Christ's righteousness?

GROWING A CHURCH WITHOUT A HEART FOR DOCTRINE

To begin with, the older I get, the less impressed I am with flashy successes and enthusiasms that are not truth-based. Everybody knows that with the right personality, the right music, the right location, and the right schedule you can grow a church without anybody really knowing what doctrinal commitments sustain it, if any. Church-planting specialists generally downplay biblical doctrine in the core values of what makes a church "successful." The long-term effect of this ethos is a weakening of the church that is concealed as long as the crowds are large, the band is loud, the tragedies are few, and persecution is still at the level of preferences.

But more and more this doctrinally-diluted brew of music, drama, life-tips, and marketing seems out of touch with real life in this world—not to mention the next. It tastes like watered-down gruel, not a nourishing meal. It simply isn't serious enough. It's too playful and chatty and casual. Its joy just doesn't feel deep enough or heartbroken or well-rooted. The injustice and perse-

---

[2] See Chapter Two, §2.3 for a description and explanation of the scope of this book.

[3] For representative literature from the voluminous literature on the gospel and law debate in the last twenty-five years, see Douglas J. Moo, "Paul and the Law in the Last Ten Years," *Scottish Journal of Theology* 40 (1987): 287-307; Stephen Westerholm, *Israel's Law and the Church's Faith: Paul and His Recent Interpreters* (Grand Rapids, MI: William B. Eerdmans, 1988); Thomas R. Schreiner, *The Law and Its Fulfillment: A Pauline Theology of Law* (Grand Rapids, MI: Baker, 1993); Frank Thielman, *Paul and the Law: A Contextual Approach* (Downers Grove, IL: InterVarsity Press, 1994); Colin G. Kruse, *Paul, the Law, and Justification* (Peabody, MA: Hendrickson, 1997); Frank Thielman, *The Law and the New Testament: The Question of Continuity,* Companions to the New Testament Series (New York: Crossroad/Herder & Herder, 1999); A. Andrew Das, *Paul, the Law, and the Covenant* (Peabody, MA: Hendrickson, 2001); Veronica Koperski, *What Are They Saying about Paul and the Law?* (New York/Mahwah, N.J.: Paulist, 2001).

cution and suffering and hellish realities in the world today are so many and so large and so close that I can't help but think that, deep inside, people are longing for something weighty and massive and rooted and stable and eternal. So it seems to me that the trifling with silly little sketches and breezy welcome-to-the-den styles on Sunday morning are just out of touch with what matters in life.

Of course, it works. Sort of. Because, in the name of felt needs, it resonates with people's impulse to run from what is most serious and weighty and what makes them most human and what might open the depths of God to their souls. The design is noble. Silliness is a stepping-stone to substance. But it's an odd path. And evidence is not ample that many are willing to move beyond fun and simplicity. So the price of minimizing truth-based joy and maximizing atmosphere-based comfort is high. More and more, it seems to me, the end might be in view. I doubt that a religious ethos with such a feel of entertainment can really survive as Christian for too many more decades. Crises reveal the cracks.

WHAT SEPTEMBER 11 REVEALED

The terrorism of September 11, 2001, released a brief tidal wave of compassion and cowardice in the Christian Church. It brought out the tender love of thousands and the terrible loss of theological nerve. "Ground Zero" became a place of agonizing comfort as Christians wept with those who wept, while radio talk shows and Muslim-Christian ecumenical gatherings became places of compromise as leaders minimized Christ and clouded the nature of Islam with vague words about "one God."

The tension between strong Christian love and weak Christological cowardice will not survive indefinitely. If the root is cut, the fruit will die—sooner or later. The reluctance to pray publicly in the majestic name of Jesus Christ; the disinclination to make clear distinctions between Allah and the God and Father of our Lord Jesus Christ;[4] the fear of drawing attention to the fact that Islam consciously rejects the entire foundation of Christian salvation, namely, the crucifixion and resurrection of Jesus[5]—this loss of conviction and courage will in the end undermine the very love and joy it aims to advance.

A DIAGNOSIS FROM WILLIAM WILBERFORCE

What we saw more clearly in the brief moment of realism following September 11 was the hidden habit of doctrinal indifference and the sad exposure of triumphant pragmatism. Surprisingly a British, evangelical politician from two hundred years ago analyzed our situation well and has helped me get my bearings in this new century. William Wilberforce is famous for his lifelong, and finally successful, battle against the African slave

---

[4] There were, thankfully, exceptions. For example, Timothy George asked, "Is the Father of Jesus the God of Muhammad?" Then he answered, "Yes and No. Yes, in the sense that the Father of Jesus is the only God there is. He is the Creator and Sovereign Lord of Muhammad, Buddha, Confucius, of every person who has ever lived. He is the one before whom all shall one day bow (Phil. 2:5-11). Christians and Muslims can together affirm many important truths about this great God—his oneness, eternity, power, majesty. As the Qur'an puts it, he is 'the Living, the Everlasting, the All-High, the All-Glorious' (2:256).

"But the answer is also No, for Muslim theology rejects the divinity of Christ and the personhood of the Holy Spirit—both essential components of the Christian understanding of God. No devout Muslim can call the God of Muhammad 'Father,' for this, to their mind, would compromise divine transcendence." Quoted from "Is the God of Muhammad the Father of Jesus?" *Christianity Today*, February 4, 2002, Vol. 46, No. 2, p. 34, which is an excerpt from George's book, *Is the Father of Jesus the God of Muhammad?* (Grand Rapids, MI: Zondervan, 2002).

[5] Thus one Sunni Muslim says, "Muslims believe that Allah saved the Messiah from the ignominy of crucifixion much as Allah saved the Seal of the Prophets from ignominy following Hijra." Badru D. Kateregga and David W. Shenk, *Islam and Christianity: A Muslim and a Christian in Dialogue* (Nairobi: Usima Press, 1980), p. 141. Hijra refers to the flight of Muhammad from Mecca in A.D. 622. It comes through Medieval Latin, from Arabic *hijrah*, literally, flight. The portion of the Qur'an that provides the basis for this denial of the crucifixion and resurrection says, ". . . and for their [the Jews'] saying: 'We slew the Messiah, Jesus son of Mary, the Messenger of God'—yet they did not slay him, neither crucified him, only a likeness of that [*shubiha lahum*] was shown to them. Those regarding him; they have no knowledge of him, except the following of surmise; and they slew him not of a certainty—no indeed; God raised him up to Him; God is All-mighty, All-wise' (4:157/156-157). Quoted from, J. Dudley Woodberry, ed., *Muslims and Christians on the Emmaus Road* (Monrovia, CA: MARC, 1989), p.165. Another Muslim witness adds, "We honor him [Jesus] more than you do. . . . Do we not honor him more than you do when we refuse to believe that God would permit him to suffer death on the cross? Rather, we believe that God took him to heaven." Quoted from a 1951 article in *The Muslim World* in J. Dudley Woodberry, ed., *Muslims and Christians on the Emmaus Road*, p. 164. Similar things are being said by Muslim clerics in the early years of this century as well. Thus one said in a church gathering soon after 9-11-01, "We believe in Jesus, more than you do in fact."

trade. It stunned me, when I recently read his one major book, *A Practical View of Christianity*, that his diagnosis of the moral weakness of Britain was doctrinal.

> The fatal habit of considering Christian morals as distinct from Christian doctrines insensibly gained strength. Thus the peculiar doctrines of Christianity went more and more out of sight, and as might naturally have been expected, the moral system itself also began to wither and decay, being robbed of that which should have supplied it with life and nutriment.[6]

Even more stunning was the fact that Wilberforce made the doctrine of justification the linchpin in his plea for moral reform in the nation. He said that all the spiritual and practical errors of the nominal Christians of his age . . .

> . . . RESULT FROM THE MISTAKEN CONCEPTION ENTERTAINED OF THE FUNDAMENTAL PRINCIPLES OF CHRISTIANITY. They consider not that Christianity is a scheme "for justifying *the ungodly*" [Romans 4:5], by Christ's dying for them "*when yet sinners*" [Romans 5:6-8], a scheme "for reconciling us to God—*when enemies*" [Romans 5:10]; and for making the fruits of holiness *the effects, not the cause*, of our being justified and reconciled.[7]

It is a remarkable thing that a politician, and a man with no formal theological education, should not only *know* the workings of God in justification and sanctification, but *consider them utterly essential* for Christian piety and public virtue. Many public people *say* that changing society requires changing people, but few show the depth of understanding Wilberforce does concerning *how* that comes about. For him the right grasp of the central doctrine of justification and its relation to sanctification—an

---

[6] William Wilberforce, *A Practical View of Christianity*, ed. Kevin Charles Belmonte (Peabody, MA: Hendrickson, 1996), p. 198.

[7] Ibid., p. 64. The SMALL CAPS is his emphasis.

emerging Christlikeness in private and public—were essential for the reformation of the morals of England.[8]

WITHOUT PASTORAL STUDY, WE LIVE ON BORROWED FAITH

If Wilberforce is right—I think he is profoundly right—it will be less of a mystery why a pastor with a burden for racial justice and the sanctity of life[9] and the moral transformation of our cultural landscape would be gripped by the doctrine of justification by faith. There are deeper and more connections than most of us realize between the grasp of doctrine and the good of people and churches and societies. The book of Romans is not prominent in the Bible for nothing. Its massive arguments are to be labored over until understood. And not just by scholars. What a tragedy that that this labor is regarded as wasted effort by so many who are giving trusted counsel in the church today.

Thousands are living on borrowed faith. We are living off the dividends, as it were, of intellectual and doctrinal investments made by pastors and church leaders from centuries ago. But the "central bank" of the Bible was not meant to fund future generations merely on the investments of the past. They are precious, and I draw on them daily. Everyone does, even those who don't know it. But without our own investments of energy in the task of understanding, the Bank will close—as it has in many churches. I had lunch with a pastor not long ago—of one of the most liberal churches in Minnesota (as he described it)—who remarked that his people would be happy if he took his text from Emily Dickinson.

---

[8] This material on Wilberforce is taken from John Piper, "'Peculiar Doctrines,' Spiritual Delight, and the Politics of Slavery," in *The Roots of Endurance: Invincible Perseverance in the Lives of John Newton, Charles Simeon, and William Wilberforce* (Wheaton, IL: Crossway Books, 2002).

[9] Abortion was a nonissue in Wilberforce's England, but frivolous death sentences were a huge issue for him; and dueling, which risked life for arrogant honor, was to him a social blight. "In the session of parliament of 1786 Wilberforce moved a bill to oppose the burning of women. In that year 20,000 people had watched the burning of Phoebe Harris outside Newgate. Wilberforce was known as a strong advocate for humanizing the penal law. Women could still be burned, after hanging for petty or high treason." John Pollock, *Wilberforce* (London: Constable, 1977), p. 41. On dueling, see ibid., p. 162.

ANSWERING THE DETAILS OF THE FIRST QUESTION: WHY DEFEND JUSTIFICATION?

So what about all those other burdens and longings I expressed in the first sentence of this chapter? Why would a pastor with all those devote so much attention to the doctrine of justification?

FOR THE SAKE OF MY FAMILY: MARRIAGE

I have a family to care for. The marriage must survive and thrive for the good of the children and the glory of Christ. God designed marriage to display the holy mercy of Christ and the happy submission of his church (Ephesians 5:21-25). My own experience has been that the doctrine of justification by faith, and the imputed righteousness of Christ, is a great marriage saver and sweetener.

What makes marriage almost impossible at times is that both partners feel so self-justified in their expectations that are not being fulfilled. There is a horrible emotional dead-end street in the words, "But it's just plain wrong for you to act that way," followed by, "That's your perfectionistic perspective," or "Do you think you do everything right?," or hopeless, resigned silence. The cycle of self-justified self-pity and anger seems unbreakable.

But what if one or both of the partners becomes overwhelmed with the truth of justification by faith alone, and with the particular truth that in Christ Jesus God credits me, for Christ's sake, as fulfilling all his expectations? What would happen if this doctrine so mastered our souls that we began to bend it from the vertical to the horizontal? What if we applied it to our marriages?

In our own imperfect efforts in this regard, there have been breakthroughs that seemed at times impossible. It is possible, for Christ's sake, to simply say, "I will no longer think merely in terms of whether my expectations are met in practice. I will, for Christ's sake, regard my wife (or husband) the way God regards me—complete and accepted in Christ—and to be helped and blessed and nurtured and cherished, even if in practice there are shortcomings." I know my wife treats me this way. And surely this is part of what Paul was calling for when he said that we should forgive "one another . . . as God in Christ forgave you" (Ephesians 4:32, ESV). I believe there is more healing for marriage in the doctrine of the imputation of Christ's righteousness than many of us have even begun to discover.

FOR THE SAKE OF MY FAMILY: CHILDREN

Then there are the children. Four sons are grown and out of the house. But they are not out of our lives. In person and on the phone every week there are major personal, relational, vocational, theological issues to deal with. In every case the root issue comes back to: What are the great truths revealed in Scripture that can give stability and guidance here? Listening and affection are crucial. But if my words lack biblical *substance*, my counsel is hollow. Touchy-feely affirmation won't cut it. Too much is at stake. These young men want rock under their feet.

My daughter, Talitha, is six years old. Recently she and my wife and I were reading through Romans together. This was her choice after we finished Acts. She is just learning to read, and I was putting my finger on each word. She stopped me in mid-sentence at the beginning of chapter 5 and asked, "What does 'justified' mean?" What do you say to a six-year-old? Do you say, "There are more important things to think about, so just trust Jesus and be a good girl"? Or do you say that it is very complex and even adults are not able to understand it fully, so you can wait and deal with it when you are older? Or do we say that it simply means that Jesus died in our place so that all our sins might be forgiven?

Or do we tell a story (which is what I did), made up on the spot, about two accused criminals, one guilty and one not guilty (one did the bad thing, and one did not do it)? The one who did not do the bad thing is shown, by all those who saw the crime, to be innocent. So the judge "justifies" him; that is, he tells him he is a law-abiding person and did not do the crime and can go free. But the other accused criminal, who really did the bad thing, is shown to be guilty, because all the people who saw the crime saw *him* do it. But then, guess what! The judge "justifies" him too and says, "I regard you as a law-abiding citizen with full rights in our country" (not just a forgiven criminal who may not be trusted or fully free in the country). At this point Talitha looks at me puzzled.

She does not know how to put her finger on the problem but senses that something is wrong here. So I say, "That's a problem, isn't it? How can a person who really did break the law and did the bad thing be told by the judge that he is a law-keeper, a righteous person, with full rights to the freedoms of the country, and doesn't have to go to jail or be punished?" She shakes her head. Then I go back to Romans 4:5 and show her that God "justifies the ungodly." Her brow is furrowed. I show her that she has sinned and I have sinned and we are all like this second criminal. And when God "justifies" us he knows we are sinners and "ungodly" and "lawbreakers." And I ask her, "What did God do so that it's right for him say to us sinners: you are not guilty, you are law-keepers in my eyes, you are righteous, and you are free to enjoy all that this country has to offer?"

She knows it has something to do with Jesus and his coming and dying in our place. That much she has learned. But what more do I tell her now? The answer to this question will depend on whether Mom and Dad have been faithfully taught about the imputation of Christ's righteousness. Will they tell her that Jesus was the perfect law-keeper and never sinned, but did everything the judge and his country expected of him? And will they tell her that when he lived and died, he not only took her place as a punishment-bearer but also stood in her place as a law-keeper? Will they say that he *was punished* for her and he *obeyed the law* for her? And if she will trust Jesus, God the Judge will let Jesus' punishment and Jesus' righteousness count for hers. So when God "justifies" her—says that she is forgiven and righteous (even though she was not punished and did not keep the law)—he does it because of Jesus. Jesus is her righteousness, and Jesus is her punishment. Trusting Jesus makes Jesus so much her Lord and Savior that he is her perfect goodness and her perfect punishment.

There are thousands of Christian families in the world who never have conversations like this. Not at six or sixteen. I don't think we have to look far then for the weakness of the church and the fun-oriented superficiality of many youth ministries and the stunning fall-out rate after high school. But how shall parents teach their children if the message they get week in and week out from the pulpit is that doctrine is unimportant? So, yes, I have a family to care for. And therefore I must understand the central doctrines of my faith—understand them so well that they can be translated for all the different ages of my children. As G. K. Chesterton once wrote, "It ought to be the oldest things that are taught to the youngest people."[10]

AND THERE ARE WEEKLY MESSAGES TO PREPARE

Which also answers why this issue matters to me when I have weekly messages to prepare and a flock to shepherd. The messages need to be saturated with biblical truth—brimming with radical relevance for the hard things in life—and helping my people be able to preach the Gospel to themselves and their children day and night. The full, rich, biblical Gospel, as it is unfolded in the New Testament and foreshadowed in the Old Testament, not as it is quickly and simply summed up in a pamphlet.[11] My people need to grow in grace and the knowledge of the Lord Jesus.[12]

---

[10] G. K. Chesterton, *What's Wrong with the World* (San Francisco, CA: Ignatius Press, 1994; orig., 1910), p. 143.

[11] And I do believe in writing pamphlets for evangelism. See *Quest for Joy: Six Biblical Truths* at www.DesiringGod.org, Topic Index, Missions and Evangelism, Quest for Joy.

[12] 2 Peter 3:18, "But grow in the grace and knowledge of our Lord and Savior Jesus Christ. To him be the glory both now and to the day of eternity. Amen."

In this way they will have strong roots for radical living, sweet comfort in times of trouble, and serious answers for their children.

JUSTIFICATION AND PRODIGALS

Then I mentioned in the first sentence of this chapter, "a personal concern for wayward children." I do not believe that even perfect parenting could prevent all wilderness wanderings of our children. Mainly because of what God said in Isaiah 1:2: "Hear, O heavens, and give ear, O earth; for the LORD has spoken: 'Children have I reared and brought up, but they have rebelled against me'" (ESV). But how do you survive and press on when a child has left the fold of God? What truth keeps you on your face in hope-full prayers and on your way to minister to others with needs as great as your own? No truth other than "the justification of the ungodly" gives as much hope for parents of a prodigal. Not only because our son or daughter may yet awaken to the hope that Christ is willing to be his or her righteousness—no matter what he or she has done—but also because the viperous guilt of failed parenting is defanged by the justification of the ungodly. Dad and Mom find a way to press on because their perfection is Christ.

JUSTIFICATION AND BIBLICAL COUNSELING

I spoke of a "love for biblical counseling." There is so much brokenness. So much sin that seems intransigently woven together with forms of failing family life and distorted personal perspectives. And it doesn't yield to quick remedies. After several decades of watching the mental health care system at work from the inside and outside, I am less hopeful about the effectiveness of (even Christian) psychotherapy than I used to be. I don't see any one strategy of helping people possessing a corner on all wisdom. But more than ever I believe the essential foundation of all healing and all Christ-exalting wholeness is a soul-penetrating grasp of the glorious truth of justification by faith, distinct from and grounding the battle for healthy, loving relationships. Good counseling patiently builds the "whole counsel" of God (Acts 20:27) into the head and heart of sinful and wounded people. And at the center of it is Christ our righteousness.

JUSTIFICATION AND A PASSION FOR WORLD EVANGELIZATION

Why devote so much time to defending the imputation of Christ's righteousness when there are so many unreached people groups and millions of people who have no access to the Gospel? I will mention two things. One is that over the past twenty years of leading a missions-mobilizing church I have seen with increasing clarity that teacher-based church planting and not just friendship-based church planting is crucial among peoples with no Christian history. In other words, doctrinal instruction becomes utterly crucial in planting the church.

This is not surprising, since embedded in the Great Commission is the command, "*teaching* them to observe all that I have commanded you" (Matthew 28:20), and since Paul planted the church in Ephesus by *reasoning daily* in the hall of Tyrannus for two years, "so that all the residents of Asia heard the word of the Lord" (Acts 19:10). In other words, it is more clear to me now that doing missions without deep doctrinal transfer through patient teaching will not only wreck on the vast reefs of ignorance but will, at best, produce weak and ever-dependent churches. Therefore, pastors who care about building, sending, and going churches must give themselves to building sending bases that breed doctrinally-deep people who are not given to emotional dependency on fads but know how to feed themselves on Christ-centered truth.

The second thing I would say about the doctrine of justification and missions is that Paul develops this doctrine in the book of Romans in a way that shows it is absolutely universal in its relevance. It crosses every culture. It is not a tribal concept. He does this by building part of the doctrine out of the connection between Adam and Christ in Romans 5:12-21. For example, take only verse 19: "For as by the one man's disobedience the many were appointed sinners, so by the one man's obedience the many will be appointed righteous." This, along with the whole context, shows that what Christ came to do in his obedience was universal in its scope and significance. It is not just for the posterity of Abraham, but for the posterity of Adam—namely, everyone.

The problem Jesus came to solve was a problem unleashed by the first man, leading to condemnation and corruption for all people everywhere in all cultures and all times. This is a stunning discovery for many people. The diagnosis of what needs to be remedied is the same in all cultures because it stems from Adam, the father of all cultures. Therefore the work of Christ to provide a "free gift of righteousness" (Romans 5:17, ESV) to all who will "receive" it is absolutely sufficient and necessary for every person in every culture everywhere in the world. And thus the doctrine of justification becomes a warrant for the universal claim of Christian missions.

TRUTH-TREASURING, BIBLE-SATURATED CHURCH PLANTING

I mentioned not only world missions but also local church planting. If I want to see churches planted out from our church and others, why invest so much time and energy in defending and explaining the historic Protestant vision of justification as the imputation of Christ's righteousness? I have answered this already but will say again, I think we have enough churches being planted by means of music, drama, creative scheduling, sprightly narrative, and marketing savvy. And there are too few that are God-centered, truth-treasuring, Bible-saturated, Christ-exalting, cross-focused, Spirit-dependent, prayer-soaked, soul-winning, justice-pursuing congregations with a wartime mindset ready to lay down their lives for the salvation of the nations and the neighborhoods. There is a blood-earnest joy that sustains a church like this, and it comes only by embracing Christ-crucified as our righteousness. As William Wilberforce said:

> If we would . . . rejoice in [Christ] as triumphantly as the first Christians did; we must learn, like them to repose our entire trust in him and to adopt the language of the apostle, "God forbid that I should glory, save in the cross of Jesus Christ" [Galatians 6:14], "who of God is made unto us wisdom and righteousness, and sanctification, and redemption" [1 Corinthians 1:30].[13]

A PASSION FOR GOD'S SUPREMACY IN ALL THINGS

Finally, I mentioned that, as a pastor and Christian, my overarching life-goal is to spread a passion for the supremacy of God in all things for the joy of all peoples through Jesus Christ. More specifically, the older I get, the more I want my life to count in the long term for the glory of Christ. That is, I want people and churches and ministries and schools to break free from the modern preoccupation with being made much of as the key to happiness and motivation and mental health and missions and almost everything else. In its place I long to see our joy—and the joy of the nations—rooted in God's wonderful work of freeing us to make much of Christ forever. There is an almost universal bondage in America to the mindset that we can only feel loved when we are made much of. The truth is, we are loved most deeply when we are helped to be free from that bondage and to find our joy in treasuring Christ and making much of him. This was Paul's passion in Philippians 1:20, "It is my eager expectation and hope that . . . now as always Christ will be honored (μεγαλυνθήσεται, *megalunthēsetai*) in my body, whether by life or by death."

This is my passion, and I pray it will be till I die. Which means that I am jealous for Christ to get all the glory he deserves in the work of justification. My concern is that in the more recent challenge to this doctrine that I am about to address he is robbed of

---

[13] Wilberforce, *A Practical View of Christianity*, p. 66.

a great part of his glory in becoming for us not only our pardon but our perfection; not only our redemption but our righteousness; not only the punishment for our disobedience but also the performer and provider of our perfect obedience. The new challenge to justification obscures (not to put it too harshly) half of Christ's glory in the work of justification.[14] It denies the imputation of Christ's righteousness and claims that there is no such teaching in the Bible.

THE TRUTH THAT MAKES THE CHURCH SING

The question must finally be answered exegetically from biblical texts, not historical precedent. That is what the major part of this book attempts. But we would be myopic not to notice that the abandonment of imputation would be a massive revision of Protestant theology and the worship of Christ. One way to illustrate this is to point out that the overthrow of the doctrine of the imputation of Christ's righteousness would involve the elimination of a great theme from our worship of Christ in song. I don't say this as an argument for the accuracy of historic exegesis, of course. I bring it in to clarify the issue and show the magnitude of it, not to settle it.

The imputed righteousness of Christ has been a great cause of joyful worship over the centuries and has informed many hymns and worship songs. The theme has cut across Calvinist-Arminian, Lutheran-Reformed, and Baptist-Presbyterian divides. As we look at some examples of hymns and worship songs, I admit that it is possible to put a different, newer meaning on some of these words, but they were not written with the newer

---

[14] "This tends to the greater glory of Christ and to our richer consolation, which they obscure and lessen not a little who detract from the price of our salvation a part of his most perfect righteousness and obedience and thus rend his seamless tunic." (Francis Turretin, *Institutes of Elenctic Theology*, Vol. 2, trans. George Musgrave Giger, ed. James T. Dennison, Jr. [Phillipsburg, NJ: Presbyterian and Reformed Publishing Company], p. 452.)

"To suppose that all Christ does is only to make atonement for us by suffering, is to make him our Savior but in part. It is to rob him of half his glory as Savior." Jonathan Edwards, *The Works of Jonathan Edwards*, Vol. 1 (Edinburgh: The Banner of Truth Trust, 1987), p. 638.

meaning, and, as a people, we would be dishonest to treat them
as if they carried the new meaning.

"AND CAN IT BE"
(CHARLES WESLEY)
No condemnation now I dread;
Jesus, and all in him, is mine!
Alive in him, my living head,
And clothed in righteousness divine,
Bold I approach the eternal throne,
And claim the crown through Christ my own.

"THE SOLID ROCK"
(EDWARD MOTE)
When he shall come with trumpet sound,
O may I then in him be found,
Dressed in his righteousness alone,
Faultless to stand before the throne.

"WE TRUST IN YOU, OUR SHIELD"
(EDITH CHERRY)
We trust in you, O Captain of salvation—
In your dear name, all other names above:
Jesus our righteousness, our sure foundation,
Our prince of glory and our king of love.

"O MYSTERY OF LOVE DIVINE"
(THOMAS GILL)
Our load of sin and misery
Didst thou, the Sinless, bear?
Thy spotless robe of purity
Do we the sinners wear?

"THY WORKS, NOT MINE, O CHRIST"
(ISAAC WATTS)
Thy righteousness, O Christ,
Alone can cover me:

No righteousness avails
Save that which is of thee.

"BEFORE THE THRONE OF GOD"
(CHARITIE LEES SMITH BANCROFT)
Behold Him there, the Risen Lamb
My perfect spotless righteousness,
The great unchangeable I am . . .

"I WILL GLORY IN MY REDEEMER"
(STEVE AND VIKKI COOK)
I will glory in my Redeemer
Who crushed the power of sin and death;
My only Savior before the holy Judge,
The Lamb Who is my righteousness.

"KNOWING YOU"
(GRAHAM KENDRICK)
Knowing you, Jesus,
Knowing you, there is no greater thing.
You're my all, you're the best,
You're my joy, my righteousness
And I love you, Lord.

We may take John Wesley for an example to support our claim that these songs are built on the historic understanding of Christ's imputed righteousness, rather than on more recent reinterpretations. Wesley himself was passionate about this doctrine, and probably more so than anywhere else in his sermon titled "The Lord Our Righteousness" (1765). He is defending himself against attacks that he did not believe this doctrine. Part of his defense is to refer to the hymns he has published. He translated Nicolaus L. Von Zinzendorf's hymn "Jesus, Thy Blood and Righteousness" and commented on it and the others he had published like this:

The Hymns . . . republished several times, (a clear testimony that my judgment was still the same,) speak full to the same purpose [of my belief in the imputed righteousness of Christ]. . . . Take one for all—

> *Jesu, thy blood and righteousness*
> *My beauty are, my glorious dress:*
> *'Midst flaming worlds in these array'd,*
> *With joy shall I lift up my head.*

"The whole hymn," he says, "expresses the same sentiment, from the beginning to the end." He goes on in this sermon to make clear what his hymns and essays mean: "To all believers the righteousness of Christ is imputed; to unbelievers it is not."[15]

From these few examples, we can see that the doctrine of the imputation of Christ's righteousness has not been experienced as marginal or minor in the worship of Christ. It has been explosive with revival power,[16] personal comfort,[17] and deep, biblically-rooted joy in worship.

---

[15] John Wesley's Sermons, Sermon #20, "The Lord Our Righteousness" (text from 1872 edition), preached at the Chapel in West-Street, Seven Dials, on Sunday, November 24, 1765. This quote was copied from http://gbgm-umc.org/umhistory/wesley/sermons/serm-020.stm#I, accessed on 3-2-02. Then, to make things as clear as possible, he quotes from his own Treatise on Justification published a year earlier (1764): "If we take the phrase of imputing Christ's righteousness, for the bestowing (as it were) the righteousness of Christ, including his obedience, as well passive as active, in the return of it, that is, in the privileges, blessings, and benefits purchased it; so a believer may be said to be justified by the righteousness of Christ imputed. The meaning is, God justifies the believer for the sake of Christ's righteousness, and not for any righteousness of his own." Further, ". . . the righteousness of Christ, both his active and passive righteousness, is the meritorious cause of our justification, and has procured for us at God's hand, that, upon our believing, we should be accounted righteous by him." Wesley's view developed over the years on this issue, but he seems to have landed in the traditional Protestant position on imputation in the latter half of his ministry, as evidenced by the sermon "The Lord Our Righteousness" (cited above) and "The Wedding Garment" (1790). For a chronological account of Wesley's view on this, see Ted M. Dorman, "Forgiveness of Past Sins: John Wesley on Justification, A Case Study Approach," *Pro Ecclesia* X/3 (Summer 2001), pp. 275-294. See also Thomas J. Nettles, "John Welsey's Contention with Calvinism: Interactions Then and Now," in *The Grace of God, the Bondage of the Will*, Vol. 2., eds. Thomas R. Schreiner and Bruce A. Ware (Grand Rapids, MI: Baker, 1995), pp. 308-309.

[16] See Chapter Two, note 2 with references to Edwards, Wesley, and Whitefield.

[17] See John Bunyan's testimony in Chapter Four, note 9.

LET CHRIST RECEIVE ALL HIS GLORY!

To magnify the glory of Christ in the fullness of his redeeming work is my aim in this book. I do not believe for a moment that any of those who represent the challenge I am opposing aim to dishonor Christ. I believe they love him and want to honor him and his Word. And I believe the mistake they are making will have the opposite effect. So for the glory of Christ and for all the reasons I have given in this chapter, I will try now to answer the arguments against the imputation of Christ's righteousness and to show from Scripture that this is part of the glory of his redeeming work.

2

THE CONTEMPORARY
CHALLENGE

§1. DEFINITION AND AIM

I begin with a definition. By *imputation* I am referring to the act in which God counts sinners to be righteousness through their faith in Christ on the basis of Christ's perfect "blood and righteousness,"[1] specifically the righteousness that Christ accomplished by his perfect obedience in life and death. My aim in this book is to give exegetical foundation to the historic Protestant teaching that the basis of our justification through faith is the provision of Christ for both pardon and imputed perfection.

In other words, I will try to show that Christ has become our substitute in two senses: in his suffering and death he becomes our curse and condemnation (Galatians 3:13; Romans 8:3). And in his suffering and life he becomes our perfection (2 Corinthians 5:21). On the one hand, his death is the climax of his atoning sufferings, which propitiate the wrath of God against us (Romans 3:24-25); on the other hand, his death is the climax of a perfect

---

[1] The phrase "blood and righteousness" is taken from Nicolaus Zinzendorf's hymn, "Jesus, Thy Blood and Righteousness."

> Jesus, thy blood and righteousness
> My beauty are, my glorious dress;
> Mid flaming worlds, in these arrayed,
> With joy shall I lift up my head.

life of righteousness imputed to us (2 Corinthians 5:21; cf. Romans 4:6, 11 with 3:21-22; 5:18-19). Along the way I will try to show why this issue is vital to the church and her mission. (See especially §4.2 and §4.3.)

The doctrine of justification is the eye of more than one storm.[2] In this book I enter only one. I am focused on the contemporary challenge to the doctrine of imputation. Is the divine righteousness, accomplished in the life and death of Jesus, imputed to us by faith alone?

§2. THREE THINGS HAVE MOVED ME TO WRITE

Besides all that I have said in Chapter One, there are several more immediate incentives that have moved me into this controversy.

---

[2] Three of the major storms, worthy of attention but not treated here, include (1) ecumenical dialogues on Evangelical and Catholic doctrine; (2) the so-called "New Perspective" on Paul and the law; and (3) the relationship of faith and obedience, specifically the conflation of faith and works of faith as the instrument of justification.

R. C. Sproul, in his book *Getting the Gospel Right: The Tie that Binds Evangelicals Together* (Grand Rapids, MI: Baker, 1999) provides a helpful history and analysis of two documents regarding Evangelical and Catholic unity ("Evangelicals and Catholics Together" and "The Gift of Salvation"). For another recent ecumenical document on justification, see *Joint Declaration on the Doctrine of Justification, The Lutheran World Federation and the Roman Catholic Church* (Grand Rapids, MI: William B. Eerdmans, 2000).

For recent responses to the New Perspective on Paul—exemplified in various ways through the writings of E. P. Sanders, James D. G. Dunn, and N. T. Wright, and not treated here—see: D. A. Carson, Peter T. O'Brien, and Mark A. Seifrid, *Justification and Variegated Nomism. Volume 1: The Complexities of Second Temple Judaism* (Tübingen: Mohr Siebeck; Grand Rapids, MI: Baker Academic, 2001); Donald A. Hagner, "Paul and Judaism: Testing the New Perspective," in Peter Stuhlmacher, *Revisiting Paul's Doctrine of Justification: A Challenge to the New Perspective* (Downers Grove, IL: InterVarsity Press, 2001); and Seyoon Kim, *Paul and the New Perspective: Second Thoughts on the Origin of Paul's Gospel* (Grand Rapids, MI: Zondervan, 2001); and Philip H. Eveson, *The Great Exchange: Justification by Faith Alone in the Light of Recent Thought* (Bromley, Kent: One Day Publications, 1996). Readers should also be aware of Mark A. Seifrid's *Christ, Our Righteousness: Paul's Theology of Justification* (Downers Grove, IL: InterVarsity Press, 2001) and Peter Stuhlmacher's *Revisiting Paul's Doctrine of Justification*.

For recent defenses of the twin pillars of justification—(1) imputation of Christ's righteousness, (2) through faith and faith alone—see Eveson, *The Great Exchange;* R. C. Sproul, *Faith Alone: The Evangelical Doctrine of Justification* (Grand Rapids, MI: Baker, 1999); and James R. White, *The God Who Justifies: The Doctrine of Justification* (Minneapolis: Bethany House, 2001). Also see the articles in the March/April issue of *Modern Reformation.*

In my view, a detailed defense still needs to be done on the historic Protestant view of the relationship between faith and obedience, so that the two are not conflated in the instrumentality of justification, as many in biblical-theological circles are doing these days. (See note 35 of Chapter Three of this book.) Perhaps, if the Lord should grant time and energy, I will take up this subject in another short book.

§2.1. Preaching Through Romans

First, I have been preaching through Romans for four years now and have arrived at chapter 8. This means that my mind and heart have been steeped in Paul's teaching on justification day and night for a long time. The effect on me has been significant. Christ himself has a more central place in my affections and my theology. His righteousness-fulfilling life (Matthew 3:15) and freely-chosen death (John 10:18) are more precious to me than ever. The doctrine of the imputation of God's righteousness in Christ has become clearer to me than ever and has proved to be a safe harbor for many of our storm-tossed people. Few things give lively comfort and lionhearted courage like the truth that Christ has fulfilled for me the demands made on me by the law of God. I am still trying to plumb the personal depths of Romans 7:4 for what it means about my dead-to-the-law relationship with Jesus Christ: "Likewise, my brothers, you also have died to the law through the body of Christ, *so that you may belong to another*, to him who has been raised from the dead, in order that we may bear fruit for God" (ESV).

§2.2. Controversy and Awakenings

Second, I have watched this doctrine of justification ignite both storms of controversy and great awakenings.[3] I have noticed that

---

[3] Jonathan Edwards wrote in 1738 after the first phase of the Great Awakening, "The beginning of the late work of God in this place, was so circumstanced that I could not but look upon it as a remarkable testimony of God's approbation of the doctrine of justification by faith alone." Jonathan Edwards, *The Great Awakening, Editor's Introduction, The Works of Jonathan Edwards,* Vol. 4 (New Haven, CT: Yale University Press, 1972), p. 19. John Wesley made the doctrine more and more central to his ministry over time (see note 15 in Chapter One). George Whitefield spoke of the doctrine of justification by faith in Christ "diligently and constantly." George Whitefield, *Select Sermons of George Whitefield* (Edinburgh: The Banner of Truth Trust, 1958), p. 54. And in a sermon on Jeremiah 23:6, titled "The Lord Our Righteousness," he said, "How the Lord is to be man's righteousness, comes next to be considered. And that is, in one word, by imputation. In that [human] nature [Christ] obeyed, and thereby fulfilled the whole moral law in our stead; and also died a painful death upon the cross, and thereby became a curse for, or instead of, those whom the Father had given to him. As God, he satisfied, at the same time that he obeyed and suffered as man; and being God and man in one person, he wrought out a full, perfect, and sufficient righteousness for all to whom it was to be imputed. Here then we see the meaning of the word righteousness. It implies the active as well as the passive obedience of the Lord Jesus Christ" (pp. 119-120).

these two are not neatly separated. It is not true, historically, that God only gives revival and awakening when the church is unified and unembattled. In the early church Paul was, it seems, fighting in almost every letter against some distortion of his Gospel *and* exulting in the truth and power of that Gospel, which was spreading rapidly in triumph and suffering. So, with a passion for reformation and revival, I long to see this precious truth of the imputed righteousness of Christ defended, known, and embraced for the salvation of souls, the good of the church, and the advancement of Christ's kingdom in the world.[4]

§2.3. A *Blast from* Books and Culture

Third, the challenge to the imputation of Christ's righteousness reached a climax for me in a very unlikely place. In two successive issues of *Books and Culture* (January/February 2001, March/April 2001, Vol. 7, Nos. 1 and 2),[5] Robert Gundry, scholar-in-residence at Westmont College, argued that "the doctrine that Christ's righteousness is imputed to believing sinners needs to be abandoned" (I, 9).[6] "That doctrine of imputation is not even biblical. Still less is it 'essential' to the Gospel" (I, 9). "The notion is passé, neither because of Roman Catholic influ-

---

[4] It is remarkable that William Wilberforce, who gave his life to overcome the slave trade in Britain, made the doctrine of justification by faith, with its clear distinction between justification and sanctification, the linchpin of his book on how England should "reform her morals" and end slavery. See William Wilberforce, *A Practical View of Christianity* (Peabody, MA: Hendrickson, 1996; orig. 1797), pp. 64, 166) and the chapter titled "William Wilberforce: 'Peculiar Doctrines,' Spiritual Delight, and the Politics of Slavery," in John Piper, *The Roots of Endurance* (Wheaton, IL: Crossway Books, 2002).

[5] Robert H. Gundry, "Why I Didn't Endorse 'The Gospel of Jesus Christ: An Evangelical Celebration' . . . Even Though I Wasn't Asked to," in *Books and Culture* (January/February 2001, Vol. 7, No. 1), pp. 6-9. Robert H. Gundry, "On Oden's Answer," in *Books and Culture* (March/April 2001, Vol. 7, No. 2), pp. 14-15, 39. This second article is a response to Thomas Oden's article, "A Calm Answer . . . to a Critique of 'The Gospel of Jesus Christ: An Evangelical Celebration" in the same issue. The two articles can be found online at http://www.christianitytoday.com/bc/2001/001/1.6.html and http://www.christianitytoday.com/bc/2001/002/4.14.html respectively. The document entitled, "The Gospel of Jesus Christ: An Evangelical Celebration," to which Gundry is responding, may be found in *Christianity Today,* June 14, 1999, pp. 51-56, and online at http://www.christianitytoday.com/ct/9t7/9t7049.html.

[6] In the body of this essay I will refer to Gundry's first article (see note 5) with a Roman numeral (I) followed by a page number, e.g., (I, 9); and the second article similarly as, for example, (II, 14).

ence nor because of theological liberalism, but because of fidelity to the relevant biblical texts" (I, 9).

These two articles by Gundry gave me the push I needed to respond, but he is not the sole or main exponent of the challenge. He simply seems to be one of the most courageous and straightforward and explicit and clearheaded. He minces no words. He puts forward the relevant evidence and lays down the challenge unlike anyone else has. But he is not alone, and he makes that plain by saying,

> I join the growing number of biblical theologians, evangelical and non-evangelical alike, who deny that Paul or any other New Testament author speaks of a righteousness of Christ (whatever it might include or exclude) that is imputed to believing sinners, and find instead a doctrine of God's righteousness as his salvific activity in a covenantal framework,[7] not in terms of an imputation of Christ's righteousness in a bookkeeping framework. (II, 15)[8]

So when I deal directly with Gundry's arguments I am not isolating him as a special case or in a class by himself. I am, by disagreement and engagement, paying him one kind of compliment: that his statement of the case is the one that gives clearest access to the challenge as a whole. Therefore I hope that the reader will not think that I have any animosity toward Dr. Gundry personally. In fact, after personal correspondence with him, in which he was willing to read and comment on the first draft of Chapter Three, I respect him with warmth and am thankful for his willingness to let me quote from his correspondence for maximum faithfulness to his intentions.

---

[7] In personal correspondence (02-04-02 quoted with permission), Gundry writes: ". . . I'm now inclined, under influence from Mark Seifrid, to drop the final phrase 'in a covenantal framework.'"

[8] He cites Mark Seifrid, Tom Wright, James Dunn, Chris Beker, and John Reumann as representatives of a newer view of justification that does not include the imputation of Christ's righteousness. "Other recognized scholars could easily be added to the list, so many in fact that it would not exaggerate to speak of a developing standard in biblical theological circles" (II, 15).

But the gulf between us on this issue is significant. Gundry's revision of the historic Protestant understanding of justification[9] goes further than his rejection of the imputation of Christ's righteousness. For example, while he does affirm "justification as a forensic declaration of believing sinners to be righteous," he does not see justification as involving *any* positive imputation to the believer of divine righteousness—whether God's or Christ's. The language of imputation (λογίζομαί, *logizomai*) relates only to "the imputation of our sins to Christ" (2 Corinthians 5:19) and "the counting of faith as righteousness" (Romans 4:5, 9, 22, 24; Galatians 3:6; James 2:23) (II, 14).

But there is even more to the challenge. Not only does Gundry regard as unbiblical any positive imputation of divine righteousness to believers, he also says that our faith itself *is* our righteousness, because God counts it to be such. "Since faith as distinct from works is credited as righteousness, the righteousness of faith is a righteousness that by God's reckoning *consists of faith* even though faith is not itself a work" (I, 8, emphasis added). But this "righteousness"—this faith—is not imputed to us, but really is our righteousness in that we respond to God in faith (by grace) and God counts our faith to be what it is—righteousness.[10] This is different from the traditional Protestant view

---

[9] For classic expositions of this traditional doctrine, see James Buchanan, *The Doctrine of Justification: An Outline of Its History in the Church and Its Exposition from Scripture* (Edinburgh: The Banner of Truth Trust, 1961; orig., 1867); John Owen, *The Doctrine of Justification by Faith*, Vol. 5 of *The Works of John Owen* (Edinburgh: The Banner of Truth Trust, 1965; orig., 1850-1853); John Murray, *Redemption—Accomplished and Applied* (Grand Rapids, MI: William B. Eerdmans, 1955), pp. 117-137.

Tom Oden has recently argued, through an examination of primary source material, that "there is a textually defined consensual classic Christian teaching on salvation by grace through faith." In other words, he endeavors to show that the classic Christian exegetes—those "pre-Protestant, pre-European, pre-medieval exegetes of the first half of the first millennium"—held to the biblical doctrine of salvation by grace through faith. See Thomas C. Oden, *The Justification Reader,* Classic Christian Readers (Grand Rapids, MI: Eerdmans, 2002), pp. 16, 23, passim.

[10] This should not be taken to mean that Gundry believes that faith is, in and of itself, righteous by its nature. In personal correspondence (02-04-02, quoted with permission), Gundry writes: ". . . I myself would rather say that God counts faith as righteousness even though it isn't righteousness in the sense of a performed work. Just as God regards believers as righteous even though they're sinners, he also regards their faith as righteousness even though it's opposite a work of moral rectitude."

that sees faith as the instrument that unites us to Christ in whom an alien righteousness, not our own, is imputed to us.

One further revision of historic Protestant teaching on justification follows from these revisions. Gundry understands justification to include liberation from slavery to sin. In other words, he blurs the distinct operations of God in justifying and sanctifying. This is not idiosyncratic, but typical of the movement he represents. On this view, justification is not purely God's bestowal of a right standing with him, but is also God's liberation of the believing sinner from the dominion of sin.

This is seen, for example, in his comments on Romans 3:24-26, where he observes that "Paul ascribes 'being justified freely by [God's] grace' to 'the redemption that is in Christ Jesus.'" Then he argues,

> Inasmuch as redemption means liberation from slavery, the language of redemption implies that here *justification does not have to do with an exchange of our sins for the righteousness of Christ; rather, it has to do with liberation from sin's mastery.* . . . God is the one whose righteousness is at stake. For sinners, it is their freedom that is at stake, so that in their case *justification translates into redemption* [i.e., liberation from slavery to sin], whereas in God's case justification translates into reputation, the maintenance of his honor. (I, 7-8, emphasis added)

§3. SUMMARY OF THE CHALLENGE TO HISTORIC PROTESTANT TEACHING

To guide my response, which follows in Chapter Three, we may sum up the proposed revisions of Protestant teaching on justification as follows, using Robert Gundry's words as representative:

§3.1. Our "faith is reckoned as righteousness" in the sense that our righteousness "consists of faith even though faith is not itself a work" (I, 8). In other words, faith, instead of receiving the

imputed righteousness of Christ, is itself our righteousness by God's decision to impute it to be so.

§3.2. Justification does not involve any positive imputation of divine righteousness (neither God's nor Christ's) to believers (II, 14).

§3.3. God's righteousness is his "salvific activity in a covenantal framework"[11] as opposed to imputation in a "bookkeeping framework." This salvific activity, called "justification," includes what has traditionally been called "sanctification": Justification "has to do with liberation from sin's mastery" (I, 7).

§3.4. The doctrine that Christ's righteousness is imputed to believing sinners needs to be abandoned as unbiblical (I, 9).

§4. Defending Imputation Is Not a Rearguard Action

§4.1. Central Reformation Battles Were Not in Vain

The cumulative effect of these revisions in the contemporary challenge, along with the claim that it is "a developing standard in biblical theological circles" (II, 15),[12] makes it hard for some of us to believe the statement that those who lift a banner today for the traditional Protestant understanding of justification are fighting "a rearguard action against a traditional Roman Catholic doctrine of justification that no longer poses a serious threat" (I, 7). It seems to us that this new challenge is precisely such a threat.

It is true that Gundry himself says explicitly, "I support the opposition to a Roman Catholic doctrine of infused righteousness" (II, 39), and that he wishes "both evangelicals and Roman Catholics . . . [would] give up their respective notions of imputation and infusion" (I, 9). But it is difficult to see how his blurring of the distinction of God's act of justification-as-declaration

---

[11] See Chapter Two, note 7.

[12] See Chapter Two, note 8 and Chapter Four, note 10.

and God's act of justification-as-liberation[13] (which I take to be historic "sanctification"[14]) is not in essence a reintroduction into justification of the *reality* of infused righteousness, if not the *language*. So it does not appear that the dispute over justification is "rearguard" at all.[15]

§4.2. The Distinction Between Justification and Sanctification Matters

It is not hard for a layperson to feel the preciousness of being counted righteous in Christ by faith alone. There are few sweeter words for a guilty sinner to hear. But the layperson may wonder if this apparent obscuring of the distinction between justification and sanctification really matters. It does. Our only hope of progress in gradual sanctification (growing in likeness to Jesus) is that we already have a right standing with God by faith alone. By this justification we are accepted into God's favor and enjoy a reconciled position. This right standing establishes the very relationship in which we find the help and power to make progress in love.

This is the very structure of salvation in the book of Romans. Precisely because "those who receive the *abundance of grace* and *the free gift of righteousness* reign in life through the one man Jesus Christ" (Romans 5:17, ESV), it seems plausible to say, "Let us sin that grace may abound" (Romans 6:1). But Paul says,

---

[13] With regard to the analysis that he "merges" these two, Gundry (02-04-02, quoted with permission) responds: "I would rather say that terms like 'justify,' 'justification,' 'righteousness,' and 'the righteousness of God' may take on different colorations of meaning in accordance with differing contexts. . . . In some contexts God's righteousness refers to salvific activity, in other contexts to retributive justice, and so on." My analysis, however, has more to do with the reality of what is happening in justification and sanctification, and not merely the linguistic differences in terms.

[14] I am using sanctification in its usual meaning of the ongoing process of being made practically holy. I am not denying that the word *hagiazō* may have wider or more nuanced meanings in the New Testament.

[15] The position of the Roman Catholic Church is stated in the official Catechism of the Catholic Church (http://www.christusrex.org/www1/CDHN/ccc.html): "Justification detaches man from sin . . . and purifies his heart of sin. . . . It frees from the enslavement to sin, and it heals" (paragraph 1990). "Justification includes the remission of sins, sanctification, and the renewal of the inner man" (paragraph 2019).

"No." Then follows his great teaching on sanctification in Romans 6 and 7. And the foundation of it is that when we were united to Christ by faith (Romans 6:5), Christ's death and righteousness became ours. We died with him, and righteousness was reckoned to us in this union. Now, and only now, can we successfully break free from our actual slavery to sinning. "We know that our old self was crucified with him in order that the body of sin might be brought to nothing, *so that* we would no longer be enslaved to sin" (Romans 6:6, ESV). A decisive death with Christ and bestowal of the "gift of righteousness" (5:17, ESV) has happened in union with Christ. Now we can joyfully and confidently fight to become what we are in Christ—free and righteous. "You also must consider yourselves dead to sin and alive to God in Christ Jesus" (Romans 6:11, ESV).

If the battle of sanctification is made part of our justification, as the newer challenge tends to make it, a great part of the foundation for triumphant warfare against sin is removed, and we are made to fight a battle that has already been fought for us and that we cannot win. Oh, there is a battle to be fought. And it is deadly. "If you live according to the flesh you will die, but if by the Spirit you put to death the deeds of the body, you will live" (Romans 8:13, ESV). "Be killing sin or [sin] will be killing you," as John Owen says.[16] But what is distinctive about the Christian warfare is that we can only kill the sin that has already been killed when we were killed in Christ. Or, to put it positively, we can only achieve practical righteousness as a working out of imputed righteousness. The battle is to become what we are in Christ: righteous with the imputed righteousness of Christ.

Yes, it matters whether the declaration of justification and the liberation of sanctification are distinguished. The battle will be engaged differently without this faith, and the fallout cannot be a happy one over the long haul.

---

[16] John Owen, *Mortification of Sin in Believers*, in *The Works of John Owen*, Vol. 6 (Edinburgh: The Banner of Truth Trust, 1967), p. 9.

§4.3. The Glory of Christ and the Care of Souls Are at Stake

Therefore, to many of us, meeting new challenges against the historic, biblical view of imputation is a front-line action rather than a rearguard action. It seems to us that the full glory of Christ is at stake as well as pastoral ministry to trembling sinners and imperfect saints.[17] We believe the Bible teaches that the saving work of Christ includes not only his bearing the penalty for our sins, but also becoming a perfect righteousness for us that is imputed to us through our union with him. If this is so, then the new challenge falls short of giving Christ all the glory due to him. And if God meant for the defiled and fearful human soul to find peace with God on the basis of Christ's "blood and righteousness," then the new challenge will profoundly affect the pastoral labor to save and comfort sinners with the Gospel.[18]

---

[17] See the Conclusion for an explanation of how the glory of Christ and the care of souls are at stake.

[18] I say this because of the, sometimes unforeseen, other significant changes in theology and pastoral counsel that come when imputation is rejected. For example, there begins to emerge a coalescing of faith and its fruit in a way that makes it difficult to counsel people how to pursue practical holiness "by faith" rather than "as faith." Some today are treating faith and obedience as two ways of speaking about one response, or as different only in their direction or intention, rather than seeing the biblical pattern that faith (as root) remains distinct from works of faith (as fruit), although never inseparable. (See the Westminster Confession of Faith, 11.2: "Faith, thus receiving and resting on Christ and His righteousness, is the alone instrument of justification: yet is it not alone in the person justified, but is ever accompanied with all other saving graces, and is no dead faith, but works by love.") Gundry does not take this step in these short articles, but others have who are following his same line of thinking. See Chapter Two, note 2 and Chapter Three, note 35.

3

AN EXEGETICAL RESPONSE TO THE CHALLENGE

In response to the four summary positions of the challenge mentioned above (Chapter Two, §3), I will try to provide "a convincing exegetical basis" for the traditional Protestant view, which Robert Gundry calls for (II, 15) rather than just a historical or theological argument.

The first two conclusions of the challenge are closely related, namely, that . . .

> . . . our "faith is reckoned as righteousness" in the sense that our righteousness "consists of faith" (I, 8, see Chapter Two, §3.1);
> . . . justification does not involve any positive imputation of divine righteousness (neither God's nor Christ's) to believers (II, 14, see Chapter Two, §3.2).

Over against these two conclusions, I argue that in the New Testament justification *does* involve a positive imputation of divine righteousness to believers (§2), and this righteousness does *not* "consist of faith," but is received by faith (§1). Paul *does* teach that God imputes to believers an external, divine righteousness, which is ours as a gift of grace.

§1. THE EVIDENCE THAT THE RIGHTEOUSNESS IMPUTED TO US IS EXTERNAL AND NOT OUR FAITH

One primary passage for consideration here is Romans 4:2-6.

> For if Abraham was justified by works, he has something to boast about, but not before God. (3) For what does the Scripture say? "Abraham believed God, and it was credited to him for righteousness" [Genesis 15:6]. (4) Now to the one who works, his wage is not credited according to grace, but according to debt. (5) But to the one who does not work, but believes in him who justifies the ungodly, his faith is credited for righteousness,[1] (6) just as David also speaks of the blessing on the man to whom God credits righteousness apart from works.[2]

§1.1. Paul Thinks of Justification in Terms of "Imputing" or "Crediting"

In Romans 4:3 Paul quotes Genesis 15:6, "Abraham believed God, and *it was credited* to him for righteousness." Thus the idea of "imputation" is introduced by the word "credited" (= "reckoned" or "counted" or "imputed"—וַיַּחְשְׁבֶהָ, *wayyaḥšᵉbehâ* and ἐλογίσθη, *elogisthē*) from Genesis 15:6. This idea of imputation or crediting is introduced in connection with Romans 4:2 to show that Abraham was not "justified by works." ("If Abraham was justified by works, he has something to boast about.")

So Paul is forging the link here between "justification" (v. 2, ἐδικαιώθη, *edikaiōthē*) and "imputation" (v. 3, ἐλογίσθη, *elogisthē*). We know, Paul says, that Abraham was not "justified" by works because Genesis 15:6 says "faith was *credited* to him for righteousness." Thus we learn that when Paul thinks of the

---

[1] Concerning the translation of ἡ πίστις εἰς δικαιοσύνην (*hē pistis eis dikaiosunēn*) as "faith for righteousness" instead of "faith as righteousness," see note 7.

[2] In most of the biblical quotations in this book the translation is my own, which may often reflect the close or even exact wording of other translations. If I do not cite an English version, I take responsibility for the translation.

justifying work of God he thinks of the *imputing* or *crediting* work of God.

How then does Paul conceive of this crediting or imputing work of God? There are clues as we consider the flow of thought through verses 4-6.

§1.2. The Context of Imputation Is One of Crediting in a Bookkeeping Metaphor

In Romans 4:4-5 Paul places the idea of imputation or crediting in the context of wages and debts. This seems to be the framework of thought that Gundry finds foreign to Paul's description of God's reckoning righteousness to our account.[3] He calls it "a bookkeeping framework" over against a "covenantal framework." But the idea of imputing or crediting or reckoning in a financial or "bookkeeping" framework seems plain in this context. The question is: How does faith relate to this act of "crediting"?

Paul's exposition of how faith relates to imputation or crediting goes like this:

> Now to the one who works, his wage is not credited/imputed (λογίζεται, logizetai) according to grace (κατὰ χάριν, kata charin), but according to debt (κατὰ ὀφείλημα, kata opheilēma). (5) But to the one who does not work, but believes in him who justifies (δικαιοῦντα, dikaiounta) the ungodly, his faith is credited/imputed (λογίζεται, logizetai) for righteousness. (Romans 4:4-5)

Immediately, something seems out of sync here with the way Gundry conceives of imputation in Romans 4:3. When Paul quotes Genesis 15:6—that "Abraham believed God, and it was credited to him for righteousness"—Gundry construes this (with

---

[3] In personal correspondence (02-04-02, quoted with permission), Gundry clarifies his view on "bookkeeping": "Though I'm still looking for any bookkeeping in regard to a righteousness of Christ, I'm quite happy with bookkeeping when it comes to the crediting of our transgressions to Christ, and to God's counting faith as righteousness."

all its parallels) to mean that Abraham's righteousness "consists of faith even though faith is not itself a work" (I, 8). So God's imputation, in Gundry's view, is not crediting an external, divine righteousness to Abraham, but counting something that he has, namely faith, to *be* his righteousness.

What seems out of sync with this interpretation is that Paul's exposition of imputation, which immediately follows verse 3, gives us a conceptual framework for imputation very different from the one Gundry sees in verse 3. Paul speaks immediately in terms of something *external* (a wage) being credited to our account, rather than something *internal* (faith) being treated as righteousness. "Now to the one who works, his wage is not credited according to grace, but according to debt." If Paul's conceptual framework were the same as Gundry's, and verse 3 implied to Paul that the credited righteousness *consists of* faith, then why would it enter Paul's mind to illustrate this with the words, "To the one who works, his wage is not credited according to grace, but according to debt"? Why would he speak in terms of a wage (or a gift) from outside ourselves being credited to us by debt (or by grace)?

Would he not rather say something like, "Now to him who works, his works are credited as (= treated as) his righteousness according to debt (κατὰ ὀφείλημα, *kata opheilēma*)"? This would correspond nicely with verse 5 ("his faith is credited for righteousness") *if* faith-credited-for-righteousness in fact means faith-treated-as-righteousness (which, I will try to show, it doesn't). Thus Paul would accomplish what Gundry seems to think he wants: to show that our righteousness consists not of our works but does *consist* of our faith. But this is *not* the conceptual framework that Paul develops. He jumps from "Abraham believed God, and it was credited to him for righteousness" (v. 3) to "a worker doesn't get his earnings according to grace but according to debt."

This seems odd and unlikely if Paul thinks about imputation

the way Gundry does. In verse 4 the very grammar is different from verse 3 and points to a different conceptual picture than Gundry's: The external reward (μισθός, *misthos*) is the subject of a passive verb ("*is credited*," μισθὸς οὐ λογίζεται, *misthos ou logizetai*) and is, therefore, the thing credited. This external reward is credited either to a "worker" as a wage "according to debt," or to "one who believes" as a gift "according to grace." Would not the wording of verse 4 rather tell us that in Paul's mind "faith being credited for righteousness" is shorthand for faith being the way an external righteousness is received as credited to us by God—namely, not by *working* but by *trusting* him who justifies the ungodly? Paul's conceptual framework for imputation in verses 4 and 5 would, therefore, not be God's crediting something *we have* to be righteousness, but God's crediting a righteousness we *don't* have to be ours by grace through faith.[4]

§1.3. Confirmation from the Connection Between Romans 4:5 and 4:6

This disconnect between Gundry's conceptual framework and Paul's is confirmed in the flow of thought between verses 5 and 6: "But to the one who does not work, but believes in him who justifies the ungodly, his faith is credited for righteousness, (6) *just as* David also speaks of the blessing on the man to whom God credits righteousness apart from works."

The "just as" at the beginning of verse 6 shows that Paul is now explaining with an Old Testament comparison (Psalm 32:1-

---

[4] So Douglas Moo, *The Epistle to the Romans,* New International Commentary on the New Testament (Grand Rapids, MI: William B. Eerdmans, 1996), p. 262.

In a helpful article on Genesis 15:6, O. Palmer Robertson points to several places in the Pentateuch where a person is "reckoned" to be something he is not. For example:

(1) Leah and Rachel ask concerning Jacob their father, "Are we not reckoned (λελογίσμεθα, *lelogismetha* LXX) by him as foreigners?" (Genesis 31:15). Leah and Rachel say that Jacob "reckons" them to be strangers when in fact they are his daughters.

(2) "Your offering shall be reckoned (λογισθήσεται, *logisthēsetai* LXX) to you as the grain of the threshing floor and as the fullness of the winepress" (Numbers 18:27: cf. v. 30). The Levite's tithe is "reckoned" as the threshing-floor corn and the fullness of the winepress though it is neither of these things.

See O. Palmer Robertson, "Genesis 15:6: New Covenant Exposition of an Old Testament Text," *WTJ* 42 (1980): 259-289.

2) what it means for God to justify the ungodly. He says, "*Just as* David also speaks of the blessing on the man to whom God credits or imputes righteousness apart from works." There are two crucial things to notice in the connection between verse 6 and verse 5.

§1.3.1. The first is the parallel between "apart from works" in verse 6 and "the ungodly" in verse 5. In verse 5 God justifies "*the ungodly.*" In verse 6 God credits righteousness to a man "*apart from works.*" What it means to be "apart from works" in Romans 4:6 is defined in verses 7-8: The man is guilty of "lawless deeds" and "sin." So God's crediting righteousness to a person "apart from works" means that he credits righteousness to "the ungodly."

§1.3.2. This leads to the second crucial thing to notice about the connection between verses 5 and 6—namely, the parallel between God's act of *justifying* in verse 5 and God's act of *crediting* or *imputing righteousness* in verse 6. We have seen that "the ungodly" in verse 5 parallels "apart from works" in verse 6. It is natural then to take the phrase, "*justify* the ungodly" to be parallel with "*credit righteousness* apart from works."

Therefore Paul thinks of *justification* of the ungodly in terms of a positive *imputation* of righteousness apart from works. And this righteousness is the direct object of the verb "credit/impute" ("[God] credits righteousness," λογίζεται δικαιοσύνην χωρὶς ἔργων, *logizetai dikaiosunēn chōris ergōn*, 4:6). Thus he is not using the same wording or grammar as in verse 5 where "faith is imputed *for* righteousness," but rather he is saying that righteousness (an objective reality outside us) is imputed to us. Justification in Paul's mind is God's imputing righteousness to us "by faith"[5] rather than faith being treated as righteousness within us.

---

[5] It is clear throughout Romans that Paul regards faith to be the instrument by which one is justified: Romans 3:28, 30; 4:11; 5:1, 2; 9:30.

§1.4. A Confirming Parallel Between Romans 4:6 and Romans 3:28

This second point is confirmed by the parallel in wording between Romans 3:28 and Romans 4:6. In Romans 3:28 Paul says, "A man is justified (δικαιοῦσθαι, *dikaiousthai*) by faith apart from works of the law (χωρὶς ἔργων νόμου, *chōris ergōn nomou*)." In Romans 4:6 he says, "God credits righteousness (λογίζεται δικαιοσύνην, *logizetai dikaiosunēn*) apart from works (χωρὶς ἔργων, *chōris ergōn*)." The parallel between "apart from works of the law" (3:28) and "apart from works" (4:6) is so close as to suggest that the other parallel between "justify" and "credits righteousness" is similarly close, even synonymous. Therefore we have another good reason for thinking that when Paul speaks of "being justified," he thinks in terms of righteousness being imputed to us rather than our faith being recognized or considered as our righteousness.

Romans 4:5	justifies	the ungodly
Romans 4:6	credits righteousness	apart from works
Romans 3:28	justified by faith	apart from works of the law

It is very important to say again here that righteousness is the *direct object* of crediting or imputing[6] (just as we saw in verse 4 that the "reward/wage" [μισθός, *misthos*] was the object of God's imputing). God imputes righteousness to a person. "David also speaks of the blessing on the man to whom *God credits righteousness apart from works.*" It does not say that God imputes something we already have (like our faith) as righteousness. It

---

[6] It is not clear whether Gundry sees this. He says, "It is our faith, not Christ's righteousness, that is credited to us as righteousness. The problem is . . . 'Celebration' attaches Christ's righteousness as a direct object of accrediting, as Paul never does. This [is an] unscriptural attachment" (II, 15). Gundry's statement is true if the focus is precisely on "Christ's righteousness"—that is, on the explicit mention of Christ. But it is not unscriptural to speak of God imputing to us a righteousness (as the direct object) that may refer to divine righteousness, including Christ's. Whether the righteousness in Romans 4:6 is in Paul's mind a divine righteousness, even Christ's, is what needs to be decided.

says that God imputes a righteousness we do not yet have because we are "ungodly."

How shall we construe the two different ways of speaking about imputed righteousness that we have seen in Romans 4:2-6? One way says, "[Faith] was credited to [Abraham] for righteousness" (4:3, 5), and the other way says, "God credits righteousness [to the ungodly] apart from works" (4:6). In the first case, faith is the thing imputed and "is imputed [by God] for righteousness" (4:5); in the second case, righteousness is the thing imputed and is imputed to us who are ungodly ("God credits righteousness apart from works," 4:6).

It is highly unlikely that Paul thinks in two different ways about how the ungodly are justified or how righteousness is imputed to the ungodly. Therefore, these two ways of speaking about imputing righteousness are probably saying the same thing in two different ways or from two different angles. The question then becomes: *What is the righteousness that God credits to the ungodly?*

Gundry answers that the righteousness credited to us by God "consists of faith even though faith is not itself a work" (I, 8). We have already argued above, from the connection between the quotation of Genesis 15:6 in Romans 4:3 and Paul's exposition of it in verses 4-5, that Gundry's answer to this question is unlikely. Gundry's conceptual framework is that the thing imputed is internal to us, namely, faith (v. 3). Paul's conceptual framework is that the thing imputed to us is external to us, namely, righteousness (v. 6). Paul's framework is that faith *receives* the gift of righteousness by trusting him who justifies the ungodly (v. 5; cf. 5:17). Gundry's framework is that faith *is* (by God's accounting) our righteousness.

§1.5. The Evidence from How Paul's Thought Flows in Romans 4:9-11

There are other lines of evidence that Paul does not intend for the phrase "faith is credited for righteousness" (4:5) to mean that our righteousness "consists of faith" (I, 8). One of these lines of evidence is the flow of thought in Romans 4:9-11.

> *Is this blessing then only for the circumcised, or also for the uncircumcised? We say that faith was credited/imputed to Abraham for righteousness. (10) How then was it credited/imputed to him? Was it before or after he had been circumcised? It was not after, but before he was circumcised. (11) He received the sign of circumcision as a seal of the righteousness of faith while he was still uncircumcised. The purpose was to make him the father of all who believe without being circumcised, so that righteousness would be counted to them.*

In verse 9 Paul uses the phrase, "faith was credited to Abraham for righteousness" (just as in verse 3). But what follows shows that Paul does *not* mean "righteousness consists of faith." Follow the flow of thought with me: After referring to faith as "credited to Abraham for righteousness" (v. 9), he asks if this crediting was before or after his circumcision (v. 10). He answers: before, not after. Then he says, "He received the sign of circumcision as a seal of the *righteousness of faith*" (v. 11). Now this term, "righteousness of faith," by itself could mean "righteousness that consists in faith" or "imputed righteousness received by faith." Which does Paul intend?

The next clause points to the answer: "The purpose was to make [Abraham] the father of all who believe without being circumcised, *so that righteousness would be counted[imputed] to them*" (εἰς τὸ λογισθῆναι αὐτοῖς δικαιοσύνην, *eis to logisthēnai autois dikaiosunēn*). Notice that Paul explains "faith being imputed for righteousness" in terms of "righteousness being imputed *because* of faith." They "believed . . . *so that* righteousness would be imputed to them." This supports our earlier conclusion that imputed righteousness is *not* "righteousness that consists in our faith," but rather "righteousness credited to us because of our faith."

§1.6. Confirming Evidence from Romans 10:10

Romans 10:10 points in the same direction. "For with the heart is believed unto righteousness, and with the mouth is confessed unto salvation" (καρδία γὰρ πιστεύεται εἰς δικαιοσύνην, στόματι δὲ ὁμολογεῖται εἰς σωτηρίαν, *kardia gar pisteuetai eis dikaiosunēn, stomati de homologeitai eis sōtērian*). Here Paul says that we believe "*unto* righteousness." And we confess "*unto* salvation." The confession does not consist in salvation but leads to it; so also the faith does not consist in righteousness but leads to it.[7]

§1.7. Evidence from Philippians 3:8-9

Another evidence that Paul does not intend for the phrase "faith is credited for righteousness" (4:5) to mean that our righteousness "consists of faith" (I, 8) is found in Philippians 3:8b-9.

> *I have suffered the loss of all things, and count them as rubbish in order that I might gain Christ, (9) and be found in him, not having a righteousness of my own from the law, but that which is through faith in Christ, the righteousness from God based on faith.*

When Paul says that he aims to be found "in [Christ], not having a righteousness of my own," does he mean that the righteousness he hopes to have in Christ is the righteousness that consists in his own faith? That is highly unlikely, because the

---

[7] Note that it would not make sense here to translate "unto" (εἰς, *eis*) by the word "as" ("with the heart is believed as righteousness"). Rather, "for" or "unto" is the natural and usual translation of this preposition, and the parallel with "with the heart is confessed unto salvation" would be broken without this normal translation. I am inclined to think that this translation should apply to Romans 4:3, 5, 9, 22 as well, since all these passages have εἰς δικαιοσύνην (*eis dikaiosunēn*) to state what faith is credited for. Hence, Romans 4:3, 5, 9, 22. should read: "faith is counted for unto righteousness," not "faith is counted as righteousness."

On a related note: Notice that "the righteousness of faith" in Romans 4:11 (τῆς δικαιοσύνης τῆς πίστεως, *tēs dikaiosunēs tēs pisteōs*) is parallel to "the from-faith righteousness" in Romans 10:6 (ἡ . . . ἐκ πίστεως δικαιοσύνη, *hē . . . ek pisteōs dikaiosunē*). This further suggests that the genitive in the phrase "righteousness of faith" should not be construed as a genitive of apposition (righteousness that is faith) but rather as a genitive of source (righteousness that comes from faith) which is similar to the phrase, "faith unto (or for) righteousness" in Romans 4:3, 5, 9, 22 and 10:10.

righteousness that he aims to have is his by virtue of being "in Christ" (ἐν αὐτῷ, *en autō*) and is said to be "*through* faith" (διὰ πίστεως, *dia pisteōs*) and "*based on* faith" (ἐπὶ τῇ πίστει, *epi tē pistei*). The conceptual framework here is not that faith *is* our righteousness, but that, because of faith, we are united to Christ in whom we have a righteousness "from God" (τὴν ἐκ θεοῦ, *tēn ek theou*). This too supports our earlier conclusion that imputed righteousness is *not* "righteousness that consists in our faith," but rather an external "righteousness credited to us because of our faith."

§1.8. A Clarifying Analogy for "Faith Imputed for Righteousness"

It might be helpful here to give an analogy that would explain how the words "faith was imputed for righteousness" can carry the meaning "faith received the gift of imputed righteousness." Don't press the following analogy in all its details. It is not an allegory.

Suppose I say to Barnabas, my teenage son, "Clean up your room before you go to school. You must have a clean room or you won't be able to go watch the game tonight." Suppose he plans poorly and leaves for school without cleaning the room. And suppose I discover the messy room and clean it. His afternoon fills up, and he gets home just before it's time to leave for the game and realizes what he has done and feels terrible. He apologizes and humbly accepts the consequences. No game.

To which I say, "Barnabas, I am going to credit the clean room to your account because of your apology and submission. Before you left for school this morning I said, 'You must have a clean room or you won't be able to go watch the game tonight.' Well, your room is clean. So you can go to the game."

That's one way to say it, which corresponds to the language of Romans 4:6. Or I could say, "I credit your apology for a clean room," which would correspond to the language of Romans 4:3. What I mean when I say, "I credit your apology for a clean room" is *not* that the apology *is* the clean room, nor that the clean room *consists of* the apology, nor that he really cleaned his room. *I* cleaned it. It was pure grace. All I mean is that, in my way of reckoning—in my grace—his apology connects him with the promise given for a clean room. The clean room is *his* clean room.

You can say it either way. Paul said it both ways: "Faith is imputed for righteousness" (4:3, 9), and "God imputes righteousness to us [by faith][8]" (4:6, 11). The reality intended in both cases is: I cleaned the room; he now has a cleaned room; he did not clean the room; he apologized for failure; in pure grace I counted his apology as connecting him with a fulfilled command that I did for him; he received the imputed obedience as a gift.

§1.9. Conclusion: Our Imputed Righteousness Does Not Consist of Faith but Is Received by Faith

So when Paul says of Abraham, or of those who believe like Abraham, that their faith "is credited for righteousness" (Romans 4:3, 5, 9, 22, 23; Galatians 3:6), he does *not* mean that righteousness "consists of faith." He simply means that their faith connects them to the promise of God's imputed righteousness.[9]

So, if we conclude thus far that Paul thinks in terms of an external righteousness credited to us, the question facing us now is: *What righteousness is credited to us? Is it God's righteousness, and possibly even Christ's?*

§2. THE EXTERNAL RIGHTEOUSNESS CREDITED TO US IS GOD'S

Now I turn to respond to the second conclusion of the new challenge to the historic Protestant view of imputation. That conclu-

---

[8] This bracket is warranted by the parallel we saw above in Chapter Three, §1.4. between Romans 4:6 and Romans 3:28.

[9] John Owen, in *The Doctrine of Justification by Faith,* Vol. 5 of *The Works of John Owen* (Edinburgh: The Banner of Truth Trust, 1965; orig., 1850-1853), pp. 318-320, gives five arguments for why "faith credited as righteousness" does not mean that faith is our righteousness. John Murray, *The Epistle to the Romans,* Vol. 1 (Grand Rapids, MI: William B. Eerdmans, 1959), pp. 353-359, gives nine arguments for the same point.

sion said, in the words of Robert Gundry, that justification does not involve any positive imputation of divine righteousness (neither God's nor Christ's) to believers (II, 14).

I have already argued that Paul does not construe the clause, "[Abraham's faith] was credited to him for righteousness" the way Gundry does—namely, that righteousness "consists of faith." Rather the wording of Romans 4:4-6 (as an exposition of that phrase) points in another direction: Faith receives the gift of an external righteousness that God credits or imputes to us.

Now what other texts support this historic interpretation, that the righteousness imputed to the ungodly in Romans 4:6 is in fact God's righteousness?

§2.1. The Flow of Thought from Romans 3:20 to 4:6

Consider first the flow of thought from Romans 3:20 into the verses we have been looking at in Romans 4:2-6. We have seen from the connection between Romans 4:3 and 4:4, on the one hand, and 4:5 and 4:6, on the other hand, that Paul conceives of *justification* in terms of an *imputation of external righteousness*. Therefore the unbroken flow of thought with regard to justification from 3:20 into chapter 4 (which I illustrate below) encourages us to think in these Pauline terms of imputation as we read Romans 3:20-22:

> *By works of the law no flesh will be justified in his sight; for through the law comes knowledge of sin. (21) But now apart from the law the righteousness of God has been manifested, being witnessed by the Law and the Prophets, (22) even the righteousness of God through faith in Jesus Christ for all who believe; for there is no distinction.*

Verse 20 announces that "*by works of the law* no flesh will be justified." This is reasserted in Romans 3:28, "We maintain that a man is justified by faith *apart from works of the law.*" Then the issue of works and justification is carried forward into

Romans 4 with the statement in verse 2, "If Abraham was *justified by works*, he has something to boast about, but not before God." So we see the unbroken chain of thought sustained from Romans 3:20 on into chapter 4 concerning justification. And here at the beginning of Romans 4 is where Paul unfolds justification as the imputation of an external righteousness.

Why is this important? Because immediately following Romans 3:20 there is a reference to the *righteousness of God*, linking it, therefore, with the righteousness that is imputed to us in justification. Paul says in Romans 3:21 that the remedy for our plight (namely, that we cannot be justified by "works") is that "the righteousness of God has been manifested." This is the solution to the fact that I cannot provide a righteousness of my own based on law. God's righteousness has been "manifested" (or as 1:17 says, "revealed").[10]

But how are we to conceive of this "manifested" divine righteousness in relationship to justification? Two things point to the answer that this divine righteousness is the very righteousness that God imputes to us when we trust in him who justifies the ungodly.

§2.1.1. First, Romans 3:21 says that this righteousness is "witnessed by the Law and the Prophets." It would be natural to take Genesis 15:6, quoted by Paul in Romans 4:3, to be an essential part of this witness since it is the main text from the Old Testament that Paul cites in this connection. But it was precisely this text that Paul unpacked in Romans 4:4-6 in terms of the imputation of an external righteousness. This points, therefore, to the conclusion that "the righteousness of God," which was witnessed to, for example, in Genesis 15:6 ("[Abraham's faith] was credited to him for righteousness") and has now been manifested as a remedy for our inability to provide a righteousness

---

[10] The same structure of thought can be seen in Romans 10:1-13. The problem is that the Jews have been seeking a righteousness based on law (v. 5). The solution is for them to submit to the righteousness based on faith (10:6, 10), which is parallel with the "righteousness of God" (10:3).

for ourselves by works, is in fact the very righteousness that, according to Romans 4:5-6, God imputes to the ungodly by faith. This conclusion is not arbitrary. It is urged by the flow of Paul's thought.

§2.1.2. But there is an even stronger argument for seeing "the righteousness of God" in Romans 3:21 as the external righteousness that is imputed to us according to Romans 4:6. Paul explicitly describes in Romans 3:22 what he means by the righteousness of God. It is "the righteousness of God *through faith in Jesus Christ for all who believe.*" In the connection of thought that we have seen between this verse and Romans 4:2-6, it is natural to see this description of God's righteousness as providing a compelling answer to the question, What righteousness is imputed to the one who has faith? Answer: the righteousness of God through faith in Jesus Christ.[11] I agree with C. E. B. Cranfield that the phrase in Romans 3:22 ("through faith in Jesus Christ," διὰ πίστεως Ἰησοῦ Χριστοῦ, *dia pisteōs Iēsou Christou*) "defines the righteousness in question as that which is received by means of faith in Christ."[12]

So we have strong contextual evidence not only that Paul conceived of justification in terms of an imputation of external righteousness, but also that he thought of this righteousness as "the

---

[11] I do not think this contradicts the truth that the righteousness of God in Romans 3:25-26 is his unwavering allegiance to uphold the worth of his glory. See John Piper, *The Justification of God* (Grand Rapids, MI: Baker Book House, 1991), pp. 135-150. There Paul says that the reason God put forth his Son to die was "as a propitiation in his blood through faith. This was to demonstrate his righteousness, because in the forbearance of God he passed over the sins previously committed; for the demonstration, I say, of his righteousness at the present time, so that he would be just and the justifier of the one who has faith in Jesus." In Paul's mind there is no conflict between speaking of God's attribute of righteousness (the unwavering commitment to uphold and display the infinite worth of his glory) and his gift of righteousness. The carrying out of God's rightness, or his justness, is his doing all things so as to express the infinite worth of his glory. This he did preeminently in the life and death of Jesus. The imputing of that righteousness to sinners is God's willingness for Christ's sake to view us as having lived with utter consistency in upholding the worth of his glory.

[12] C. E. B. Cranfield, *The Epistle to the Romans*, ICC, Vol. 1 (Edinburgh: T. & T. Clark Ltd., 1975), p. 203. Cranfield argues successfully, I think, for construing the genitive of Ἰησοῦ Χριστοῦ (*Iēsou Christou*) as the object of faith rather than as "faithfulness of Jesus Christ." On construing Ἰησοῦ Χριστοῦ (*Iēsou Christou*), see also Thomas R. Schreiner, *Romans*, Baker Exegetical Commentary on the New Testament (Grand Rapids, MI: Baker Books, 1998), pp. 181-186; Douglas Moo, *The Epistle to the Romans*, pp. 224-226.

righteousness of God" that has been manifested now through the work of Christ and is received through faith as the remedy for us who cannot perform our own righteousness by works of the law. God reveals his own righteousness that we receive through free and gracious imputation by faith. Whether there is exegetical warrant for construing God's righteousness as also Christ's righteousness will be discussed below in §4.

§2.2. The Evidence for Imputed Divine Righteousness in 2 Corinthians 5:21

Another evidence that Paul thought in terms of an imputed external divine righteousness of God is found in 2 Corinthians 5:21, ESV, "For our sake [God] made [Christ] to be sin[13] who knew no sin, so that in him we might become the righteousness of God." Gundry's handling of this text acknowledges, in vague terms, that "God's righteousness . . . comes into play as a result of union with Christ."

> Whatever it means to "become" the righteousness of God in Christ, the point remains that it is God's righteousness, not that of Christ, which comes into play as a result of union with Christ. Apart from the imputation of transgressions to Christ [2 Corinthians 5:19], Paul uses the language of union, reconciliation, being made, and becoming rather than the language of imputation. (I, 7)

But the question is not about mere explicitness of "language" (like "comes into play") but about the *reality* revealed through language. In view of all we have seen from Romans 3 and 4, it is not unnatural or contrived to see in the words "in [Christ] we . . .

---

[13] The translation "sin offering" ("God made him to be a sin offering"), preferred by some modern commentators, is unlikely given that the word "sin" in the phrase "who knew no sin" (τὸν μὴ γνόντα ἁμαρτίαν, *ton mē gnonta hamartian*) cannot refer to a sin offering. (Cf. Paul Barnett, *The Second Epistle to the Corinthians*, The New International Commentary on the New Testament [Grand Rapids, MI: William B. Eerdmans, 1997], p. 314, n. 65.) This would apply to Romans 8:3 as well, contra the NASB translation (". . . sending His own Son in the likeness of sinful flesh and as an offering for sin").

become the righteousness of God" a reference to the imputation of God's righteousness to us.

This is not a mere guess. It follows from the parallel with Christ's being "made sin" for us. Christ is "made sin" not in the sense that he *becomes* a sinner, but in the sense that our sins are imputed to him—a natural interpretation in view of the explicit reference in 2 Corinthians 5:19 to God's "not imputing" (μὴ λογι-ζόμενος, *mē logizomenos*) trespasses. In other words, the concept of "imputation" is in Paul's mind as he writes these verses.

But if Christ's being made sin for us implies the imputation of our sin to Christ, then it is not arbitrary or unnatural to construe the parallel—our "becoming the righteousness of God in him"—as the imputation of God's righteousness to us. We "become" God's righteousness the way Christ "was made" our sin. *He* did not become morally sinful in the imputation; *we* do not become morally righteous in the imputation. *He* was counted as having our sin; *we* are counted as having God's righteousness. This is the reality of imputation. And the righteousness imputed is not our faith but an external divine righteousness.

§2.3. Conclusion: God Imputes His Righteousness to Us Through Faith

In conclusion then, on this second point of response to the challenge, I affirm again that, in the New Testament, justification *does* involve a positive imputation of divine righteousness to believers, and this righteousness does *not* "consist of faith" but is received by faith. Paul *does* teach that God imputes to believers an external, divine righteousness that is ours as a gift of grace. This conclusion, I have tried to show, is the fruit of exegesis, not the imposition onto the Bible of foreign ideas.

§3. JUSTIFICATION IS NOT LIBERATION FROM SIN'S MASTERY

Now we take up the third part of the challenge to the historic Protestant view of justification. Robert Gundry expressed it by saying that God's righteousness is his "salvific activity in a covenantal framework"[14] as opposed to imputation in a "bookkeeping framework." Thus this salvific activity, called "justification," includes what has traditionally been called "sanctification." Justification, Gundry says, "has to do with liberation from sin's mastery" (I, 7).

§3.1. A Controlling Biblical-Theological Paradigm?

This part of the challenge to the historical position represents a paradigm that exerts as much power in biblical theology today as covenant theology sometimes does in systematic theology. It is represented by Gundry's statement that God's righteousness is his "salvific activity in a covenantal framework" as opposed to imputation in a "bookkeeping framework." One of the troubling things about this "developing standard in biblical theological circles" (II, 15)[15] is that it is generally expressed in the same vague and general ways that make systematic categories so annoying to exegetes. In other words, it bears all the marks of a widespread scholarly paradigm that exerts a controlling effect on the exegesis of texts that do not clearly support it.[16]

The idea is difficult to falsify because it is so broad and vague ("salvific activity") that almost anything God does can be included in it—even punitive judgment, if the punishment is seen as judgment on the enemies of God's people and thus "salvific" for the elect.[17] One of the signals that the paradigm has over-

---

[14] See Chapter Two, note 7.

[15] See Chapter Two, note 8 and Chapter Four, note 10.

[16] It is of deep concern to me that this move away from the historic Protestant view on justification is bringing in its wake a tendency to sacrifice clarity and definition in discussions of justification by faith (a tendency of which Robert Gundry is generally not guilty, which makes him the likeliest candidate to respond to). There is a tendency to use the familiar language of historic Protestantism, but with new content. There is great hesitancy to make clear to the readers or listeners that the content is new. I think that those who are moving in this direction have some sense of the magnitude of their defection from mainstream Protestantism and are anxious about the repercussions of such a doctrinal revision. This is a dangerous tendency and begins to erode the importance of truth and clarity—what Paul described as "refusing to practice cunning or to tamper with God's word, but by the open statement of the truth we would commend ourselves to everyone's conscience in the sight of God" (2 Corinthians 4:2).

[17] I have tried to show elsewhere that the contemporary tendency to see God's righteousness as saving only and not also including wrath and judgment is wrong. Piper, *The Justification of God*, pp. 108-122. See Lamentations 1:18; Isaiah 5:16; 10:22; Nehemiah 9:33.

stepped its bounds is that it leads some interpreters to see broad references to God's liberating activity (traditionally called sanctification) in some of Paul's carefully-worded statements about justification. I think Gundry moves in this direction. For he says justification "has to do with liberation from sin's mastery" (I, 7).

I would argue that justification in Paul's thinking consistently refers to God's declaring sinners to be righteous who trust Christ, and that it never refers to God's sanctifying or purifying activity. I am not saying here that Paul never uses the δικαι- word group to refer to practical moral charge. I am saying that the word δικαιόω consistently means "justify" in the declarative sense, not "purify" in the transformational sense. In a profound sense God's justifying act is "salvific" and is foundational and preparatory for all of God's subsequent sanctifying work by which we are liberated from sin's mastery. So the two works of God (justification and sanctification) are closely connected, and in the broadest sense justification "has to do with" liberation from sin's mastery. It "has to do with" it in the sense that justification gives the foundation of a right standing before God, through the imputation of divine righteousness, which is then followed by the blessings that come to a justified sinner, including the liberating, sanctifying work of God's Spirit.

But Gundry means something very different than this, as he shows from the way he deals with Romans 3:24-26.

> . . . *being justified as a gift by his grace through the redemption that is in Christ Jesus; (25) whom God put forward as a propitiation in his blood through faith. This was to demonstrate his righteousness, on account of the passing over of sins previously committed; (26) in the forebearance of God—for the demonstration of his righteousness at the present time, so that he might be just and the justifier of the one who has faith in Jesus.*

Commenting on the words, "justified . . . through the redemption that is in Christ Jesus," Gundry says, "Paul ascribes 'being justified freely by [God's] grace' to 'the redemption that is in Christ Jesus.'" Then he draws this inference from the concept of "redemption":

> Inasmuch as redemption means liberation from slavery, the language of redemption implies that here *justification does not have to do with an exchange of our sins for the righteousness of Christ; rather, it has to do with liberation from sin's mastery* (contrast God's giving human beings over to various forms of evil in 1:24, 26, 28; and compare 6:6-7, which speaks of having been justified "from sin" as opposed to enslavement to sin—also 6:15-23; 7:7-25). (I, 7-8, emphasis added)

From this, Gundry infers that "justification translates into redemption," which he has defined as "liberation from slavery." So Gundry means much more than a broad general statement that justification "has to do with" liberation from sin's mastery (sanctification); rather he means that justification "translates into" redemption, which "means liberation from slavery [to sin]."

Therefore I assume Gundry would agree with Peter Stuhlmacher's conclusion that "the dogmatic distinction . . . between a justification which is first only reckoned legally (forensic-imputed) and a justification which is creatively at work (effective [= sanctification]) is . . . an unbiblical abstraction."[18] Both are speaking from the scholarly paradigm that carries one from the righteousness of God as "salvific activity"—especially liberating activity—to the understanding of justification as effective liberation from the mastery of sin.[19]

---

[18] Peter Stuhlmacher, *Paul's Letter to the Romans: A Commentary*, trans. Scott J. Hafemann (Louisville: Westminster/John Knox Press, 1994), pp. 63-64. This is not a misprint: "justification" is used twice. The second use is what is traditionally taken to mean sanctification.

[19] Ibid., p. 31: "In the Old Testament, in the early Jewish tradition, and in the New Testament, God's righteousness thus means the salvific activity of God the creator and judge, who creates for those concerned righteousness and well-being."

§3.2. Does the New Paradigm Do Justice to Romans 3:24-26?

The textual support for Gundry's and Stuhlmacher's viewpoint does not carry the weight of the claim. Gundry builds his case on the meaning of "redemption" in Romans 3:24 as "liberation from slavery." But the word "redemption" can refer to different kinds of rescues (e.g., from groaning bodies, Romans 8:23; or from the guilt of sin, Ephesians 1:7; Colossians 1:14). The fact that it is a large concept reminds us that every aspect of a concept need not be in view each time a word is mentioned. What is Paul's particular meaning of "redemption" here in Romans 3:24?

The closest parallels to Paul's use of "redemption" in Romans 3:24 are Ephesians 1:7 ("In him we have redemption through his blood, *the forgiveness of our trespasses*, according to the riches of his grace") and Colossians 1:14 (". . . in whom we have redemption, *the forgiveness of sins*").[20] In both these texts the focus is on redemption as forgiveness, not as the sanctifying deliverance from the power of sin.[21] That is the way I understand the meaning in Romans 3:24. This is confirmed by Romans 3:25 where the propitiation mentioned is necessary on account of "the passing over of sins previously committed." The issue in Romans 3:24-26 is how God can pass over sins (past, present, and future), not how God can transform sinners. The answer is through pro-

---

[20] Conceptually related to "redemption" (ἀπολύτρωσις, *apolutrōsis*) are the terms "ransom" (λύτρον, *lutron*) and "purchase" (ἀγοράζω, *agorazō*). These terms all have a legal background to them. For more on this, see Herman Ridderbos, *Paul: An Outline of His Theology*, trans. John Richard DeWitt (Grand Rapids, MI: William B. Eerdmans, 1975), pp. 193-197. See also Leon Morris, *Apostolic Preaching of the Cross*, third revised edition (Grand Rapids, MI: William B. Eerdmans, 1965), pp. 12-13, who notes, "It is important to realize that it is this idea of payment as the basis of release which is the reason for the existence of the whole word group. . . . The very existence of this word-group is due to the desire to give precise expression to the conception of release by payment. There is thus a *prima facie* case for holding that the redemption terminology is concerned with the price-paying method of release." He concludes, "The actual usage of ἀπολύτρωσις [*apolutrōsis*] shows 'ransoming' rather than 'deliverance' to be the essential meaning of the word" (p. 41).

[21] Consider Galatians 3:13 where Paul tells us that "Christ redeemed (ἐξηγόρασεν, *exēgorasen*) us from the curse of the law by becoming a curse for us." The focus of our redemption again is on our guilt and condemnation that the law brings, not first on our slavery to sinning.

pitiation by the blood of Christ, and the effect is "redemption"—that is, sins are really passed over and forgiven.

Here, it seems, we see the danger of a "biblical-theological"
paradigm working to silence the particularity of a text's meaning. It is not just "dogmatic categories" that function this way.
So do ruling paradigms in "biblical theology." What is happening in Romans 3:24-26 is that "the righteousness of God,"
understood broadly from the Old Testament and Jewish literature as God's "salvific activity," is exerting more influence than
the particularities of the text.

The way this paradigm seems to function is that, first, one
observes from the Old Testament that "redemption" sometimes
refers to the rescuing acts of God (like the Exodus). Then one
aligns this "salvific activity" with "the righteousness of God."
Then one brings all of that to Romans 3:24-26, thus making the
cross a demonstration of God's righteousness in the sense that it
is God's "salvific activity" in which he liberates his people in a
second exodus from the guilt *and the power* of sin.

But what this does is obscure the point that the righteousness
of God in Romans 3:24-26 is at issue *not* because people are in
bondage to sin, but because God has passed over sin.
Righteousness in this paragraph does not simply point to God's
"salvific activity," but specifically to the demand of God's justice
not to acquit the guilty. The righteousness of God in this paragraph is in question because real sins are being passed over, and
guilty sinners seem to have simply been acquitted. This would be
an abomination by God's standards of righteousness (Proverbs
17:15, "He who justifies the wicked and he who condemns the
righteous are both alike an abomination to the LORD," ESV)

This is almost the exact opposite of seeing God's righteousness as "salvific activity." In Romans 3:24-26 God's righteousness is calling God's salvific activity into question. God's
righteousness is not the thing that is pressing for salvation. In
these verses righteousness is making a very particular contribu-

tion to salvation—namely, substitution will be required. It is this huge particularity in the text that gets lost in the sweeping statements about righteousness as "salvific activity." It is against this backdrop of particular meaning in *this* text that "redemption" is to be understood.

§3.3. How the New Paradigm Mishandles Justification in Romans 6:6-7

Besides Romans 3:24-26, the new paradigm sees justification as liberation from actual sinning in Romans 6:6-7: "Our old self was crucified with him in order that the body of sin might be done away with, so that we would no longer be enslaved to sin; (7) for he who has died *has been justified from sin* (δεδικαίωται ἀπὸ τῆς ἁμαρτίας, *dedikaiōtai apo tēs hamartias*)." Gundry says that verse 7 "speaks of having been justified 'from sin' as opposed to enslavement to sin" (I, 7-8). In other words, Gundry thinks that Romans 6:6-7 implies that justification is a liberation from slavery to sin—that is, it overlaps with sanctification.

But these verses will not sustain this interpretation. Verse 7 is the ground for verse 6 (see the γὰρ [*gar*] at the beginning of verse 7). It supports verse 6, which says that our old man died with Christ so that we might no longer serve sin. The question is: *How* does verse 7 ground verse 6? Does it ground it by saying that when you die with Christ you are *freed* from sinning? Or does it ground verse 6 by saying that when you die with Christ, you are freed from the guilt and condemnation of sin—that is, that you are justified and acquitted from sin and now have a right standing with God?

§3.3.1. THE MEANING OF "JUSTIFIED FROM SIN" IN ROMANS 6:7

There is no reason for Gundry to assume (as he seems to) that "justification from sin" (v. 7) means liberation from the mastery of sin, when in fact it may refer to the indispensable *foundation* for that subsequent liberation. It may be that justification—as declaration of freedom from guilt and condemnation—is that without which we could not even get started in the battle against sin's dominion. A parallel in Acts 13:38-39 shows that the phrase, "justified from" (δεδικαίωται ἀπό, *dedikaiōtai apo*) can mean "acquitted from" or "forgiven for," rather than "liberated from."

> *Therefore let it be known to you, brothers, that through him forgiveness of sins is proclaimed to you, (39) and by him everyone who believes is justified (δικαιοῦται, dikaioutai) from all things (ἀπὸ πάντων, apo pantōn), from which you could not be justified (δικαιωθῆναι, dikaiōthēnai) by the Law of Moses. (Acts 13:38-39)*

The context of "forgiveness" (v. 38) shows that the meaning of "being justified" here is not an ethical sense of "being freed from sin's power," but a forensic sense of "being justified or acquitted from sin's guilt." So Romans 6:7, with its similar wording, is likely to have this meaning. If so, the point of verse 7 would be to give not a definition but a *ground* for the ethical transformation in verse 6. The ground for no longer being enslaved to sin (v. 6) is our justified standing with God (v. 7).

This is the meaning we should give the passage because the ordinary meaning of the word "justify" (δικαιόω, *dikaioō*) is "to pronounce just," not "to make just" and not "to liberate from sin." "The verb denotes the giving of the verdict whereby [people] are adjudged righteous or acceptable with God."[22] It simply does not mean "liberate," and to give it such an unusual meaning would require overwhelming contextual demands, which are not present.

§3.3.2. ANOTHER WAY TO UNDERSTAND ROMANS 6:6-7

In fact, not only does the word "justify" (δικαιόω, *dikaioō*) not allow, and the context not demand, the meaning "liberate," but

---

[22] Morris, *The Apostolic Preaching of the Cross*, p. 285.

I would argue that the context and the spiritual nature of bondage to sin plead for the very meaning for "justify" that it always has, "declare righteous." That is, I would argue that God's imputed righteousness, and our right standing with God, over against our sin (Romans 6:7) is the clear and distinct and necessary ground for sanctification—our liberation from sin (v. 6, "no longer enslaved to sin").

§3.3.2.1. First, contextually, this is the very structure of Paul's argument in Romans as he moves from chapters 3—5 into chapter 6. The doctrine of justification by faith apart from works (3:28) raises the question, "Are we to continue in sin that grace may increase?" (Romans 6:1). And: "Shall we sin because we are not under law but under grace?" (Romans 6:15). The raising of these questions is a powerful indication that justification does *not* include liberation from the mastery of sin. For if it did, these questions would not plausibly arise. If Paul had just spent three chapters teaching that justification means God's powerful salvific activity in liberating people from the mastery of sin, why would the question arise: So shall we sin that grace may abound?[23]

It is not in the least plausible to object, "Well, Paul, if justification is the work of God's grace to liberate us from sin, then let us sin that this grace may abound." No, what gives some measure of plausibility to these rhetorical questions in Romans 6:1 and 6:15 is the doctrine of Romans 3—5 that justification is emphatically *not* liberation from the mastery of sin. It does *not*

---

[23] In personal correspondence (02-04-02, quoted with permission), Gundry writes: "But I don't say that in the chapters preceding Romans 6 Paul has been presenting justification as liberation from the mastery of sin, or deny that in those chapters he has been arguing for forensic justification. He certainly has been arguing for forensic justification. I do affirm, however, that when that argument raises the question of sinning that grace may abound, Paul extends justification—at this point (Romans 6:6-7)—to include liberation from enslavement to sin." But see above, Chapter Two, §2.3 and Chapter Three, §3.1 where Gundry argues from Romans 3:24-26 that "justification translates into redemption," which he has defined as "liberation from slavery." He writes the following with regard to Romans 3:24-26, ". . . here justification does not have to do with an exchange of our sins for the righteousness of Christ; rather, it has to do with liberation from sin's mastery . . . justification translates into redemption [i.e., liberation from slavery to sin] . . ." (I, 7-8, emphasis added). I don't see how this fits with Gundry's statement that he has not said that Romans 1—5 has to do with justification as liberation from sin.

include sanctification. That is precisely what creates the need for Paul to write Romans 6—8: to show why God's imputing his own righteousness to us by faith apart from works does not result in lawlessness, but in fact necessarily leads to righteous living. Therefore we are not at all encouraged to blur the relationship between sanctification and justification that Paul preserves in Romans 6:6-7: Justification is the necessary and prior basis of sanctification ("for," v. 7).

§3.3.2.2. Moreover, the spiritual nature of bondage to sin points to this same conclusion. The word "because" or "for" connecting Romans 6:6 and 7 shows that Paul sees the justification of verse 7 as a logical ground or basis of the sanctification of verse 6.[24] To understand this connection and the role of justification in grounding sanctification, we may ask: How does sin enslave? If it enslaves *only* by its alluring power, then the natural interpretation of verse 7 might be that our dying with Christ "frees" (rather than justifies us) us from the power of sin and *therefore* overcomes slavery to sin (v. 6).

But there is another way that sin enslaves, namely, by its guilt. This is less obvious and perhaps more insidious and powerful. I see it implied in the phrase "*justified* from sin," and I have seen it in people in real life. What I mean is this: Sin creates a real guilt that makes a person feel despairing and hopeless. That despair and hopelessness is one of the most powerful bondages to sinning there is. You ask such people if they know that the sin's lure is a lie, and they will, amazingly, agree with you that it is a lie. But they feel hopeless and therefore say, "It doesn't matter, there's no hope anyway; I am beyond forgiveness." This is a very deep bondage to actual sinning rooted in the despair of guilt. I would

---

[24] Note that verses 6-7 seem analogous to verse 14: "For sin shall not be master over you, for you are not under law but under grace." Notice how the phrase, "sin shall not be master over you" (v. 14) corresponds to "that we should no longer be slaves of sin" (v. 6); and the phrase "for he who has died is justified from sin" (v. 7) corresponds to "for you are not under law, but under grace" (v. 14). The phrase, "not under law," is clearly forensic, not transformative (because of the argument developed in §3.3.2.1), which would thus confirm that the parallel "justified from sin" is forensic also; that is, it means, "acquitted and declared righteous over against the indictment of sin."

argue that this kind of bondage is precisely what verse 7 can over-come—and is probably designed to overcome. Justification—legal acquittal from sin and the declaration of our righteousness before God—grounds the possibility of liberation from slavery to sin. In wakening hope for acceptance with God by faith alone, it creates the very possibility and foundation for fighting against the bondage of sin that enslaves us. Therefore keeping the natural meaning, "justify," for δεδικαίωται (*dedikaiōtai*) in verse 7 is both exegetically warranted and existentially crucial.

§3.4. The Flow of Thought in Romans 8:3-4

This understanding of the relationship between justification and sanctification in Romans 6:6-7 is supported by the flow of thought in Romans 8:3-4.

> *For what the law could not do, weak as it was through the flesh, God did: sending his own Son in the likeness of sinful flesh and for sin, he condemned sin in the flesh, (4) in order that the righteous requirement of the law might be fulfilled in us, who walk not according to the flesh but according to the Spirit.*

The word "condemned" in Romans 8:3 recalls the words from verse 1, "There is no *condemnation* for those who are in Christ Jesus." This is a reference to the reality of justification. ("Who shall bring any charge against God's elect? It is God who *justifies*. Who is to *condemn*?" [Romans 8:33-34, ESV].) The Son of God became flesh so that the "condemnation" of sin might be on him (who had no sin). That is, he bore our condemnation. We are now viewed as free from condemnation "in Christ" (v. 1) when we are united to him by faith.

Now what is the relationship between this justified state and our being freed from the slavery of sin (sanctification)? Verse 4 describes the fulfillment of the law "*in* us" (not just *for* us), and therefore refers to the real practical progress of sanctification (". . . in order that the righteous requirement of the law might be

fulfilled in us, who walk not according to the flesh but according to the Spirit").[25] The logical relationship with verse 3 (justification) is that verse 4 (sanctification) *results from* and is the
purpose of verse 3. "(3) [God] condemned sin in the flesh, (4) *so
that* the requirement of the law might be fulfilled in us." In other
words, our union with Christ in his death for us secures our *justification,* which then leads, as a result, to our moral *transformation.* This is the same logic we saw in Romans 6:6-7. We were
crucified with Christ so that we might not serve sin (v. 6), *because*
the one who has died is justified from sin (v. 7), and on the basis
of that justification, moral transformation becomes possible.

§3.5 Conclusion: Justification Is Not Liberation from Sin's Mastery

In conclusion, then, the assault on the historic distinction
between justification and sanctification does not seem to me to
be successful. I find no exegetical warrant for allowing the vague
and general designation of the righteousness of God as "salvific
activity" to lead us away from the traditional understanding of
justification as the imputation of divine righteousness. And I see
no exegetical warrant for construing justification so as to include
"liberation from sin's mastery." Gundry's arguments do not
overthrow the traditional Protestant understanding of Scripture
that finds in justification the imputation of divine righteousness
and a clear and necessary distinction between this act and God's
subsequent and necessary work of sanctification.

§4. IS THE DIVINE RIGHTEOUSNESS THAT IS IMPUTED TO BELIEVERS THE RIGHTEOUSNESS OF CHRIST?

The fourth part of the challenge against the historic Protestant
view of imputation is that there is no teaching in the New
Testament concerning the imputation of *Christ's* righteousness.

---

[25] So Schreiner, *Romans,* pp. 404-407; contra Moo, *The Epistle to the Romans,* pp. 482-485.

In Robert Gundry's words, "The doctrine that Christ's righteousness is imputed to believing sinners needs to be abandoned as unbiblical" (I, 9). Is this true? Or to ask the question differently, Can the divine righteousness imputed to believers (which we have argued for above in §3.2) properly be identified as *Christ's* righteousness? In particular, is this righteousness his incarnate obedience to God?

Before dealing in some detail with the key passage in Romans 5:12-19, I will take up four texts that point toward the imputation of Christ's righteousness.

§4.1. The Evidence for the Imputation of Christ's Righteousness from 2 Corinthians 5:21

Second Corinthians 5:21 is one of the most powerful statements on the reality of an external divine righteousness imputed to believers. "[God] made [Christ] who knew no sin to be sin on our behalf, so that we might become the righteousness of God in him." What is crucial to focus on here is the parallel between the two halves of the verse. Charles Hodge points to the parallel when he says, "His being made sin is consistent with his being in himself free from sin; and our being made righteous is consistent with our being in ourselves ungodly."[26]

What is so illuminating here is specifically the parallel between Christ's being "made sin" and our "becoming righteous." George Ladd brings this out with its crucial implication for imputation.

> Christ was made sin for our sake. We might say that our sins were reckoned to Christ. He, although sinless, identified himself with our sins, suffered their penalty and doom—death. So we

---

[26] Charles Hodge, *An Exposition of the Second Letter to the Corinthians* (Grand Rapids, MI: William B. Eerdmans, n.d.), p. 149. Hodge knows that "Paul never expressly states that the righteousness of Christ is reckoned to believers" (p. 148). But his conclusion shows that the absence of doctrinal explicitness and systematization in Paul may be no more problematic for the doctrine of the imputation of Christ's righteousness than it is for the doctrine of the Trinity.

have reckoned to us Christ's righteousness even though in character and deed we remain sinners. It is an unavoidable logical conclusion that men of faith are justified because Christ's righteousness is imputed to them.[27]

Gundry, on the other hand, observes that

what jumps out is that this passage distinguishes Christ from God and mentions "the righteousness of God" but not any righteousness of Christ, only his innocence. . . . Nothing is said about an imputation of his sinlessness, however, or about his righteousness, which goes unmentioned and therefore is not said to be imputed. (I, 7)

True, this text does not say explicitly that *Christ's* righteousness is imputed to believers. But it does say that believers, because they are "in Christ," become God's righteousness the way Christ was made sin as a sinless person. It does not seem to me like an artificial category of systematic theology imported from outside the Bible to argue like this: 1) The combination of divine righteousness being ours the way sin was Christ's, together with 2) the fact that this divine righteousness is ours only "in Christ," together with 3) the close parallel in Romans 5:19 ("Through the obedience of the One the many will be appointed[28] righteous")—these three things together lead to the conclusion that the imputation of Christ's perfect righteousness was credited to our account, as our sin was credited to his account in the penal suffering he endured in our place.

I don't know a better summary of the implications of 2 Corinthians 5:21 than the words of Charles Hodge:

There is probably no passage in the Scriptures in which the doctrine of justification is more concisely or clearly stated than in

---

[27] George Ladd, *A Theology of the New Testament,* revised, ed. Donald Hagner (Grand Rapids, MI: William B. Eerdmans, 1993), p. 491.

[28] See the treatment of this verse and this word below in §4.5.4 and notes 51-56.

[2 Corinthians 5:21]. Our sins were imputed to Christ, and his righteousness is imputed to us. He bore our sins; we are clothed in his righteousness. . . . Christ bearing our sins did not make him morally a sinner . . . nor does Christ's righteousness become subjectively ours, it is not the moral quality of our souls. . . . Our sins were the judicial ground of the sufferings of Christ, so that they were a satisfaction of justice; and his righteousness is the judicial ground of our acceptance with God, so that our pardon is an act of justice. . . . It is not mere pardon, but justification alone, that gives us peace with God.[29]

In other words, this text gives us biblical warrant for believing that the divine righteousness that we saw imputed to believers in Romans 4:6 and 11 (see above) is the righteousness of Christ.

§4.2. The Evidence for the Imputation of Christ's Righteousness from Philippians 3:9

Philippians 3:9 speaks of a righteousness that Paul "has" (ἔχων, *exōn*) that is "not his own" (μὴ . . . ἐμήν, *mē . . . emēn*) and that "comes from God" (τὴν ἐκ θεοῦ δικαιοσύνην, *tēn ek theou dikaiosunēn*) because we are "in Christ" (ἐν αὐτῷ, *en autō*).

I count all things to be . . . rubbish so that I may gain Christ,
(9) and may be found in him, not having a righteousness of my
own derived from the law, but that which is through faith in
Christ, the righteousness which comes from God on the basis
of faith. (Philippians 3:8-9)

Gundry again simply observes that the righteousness of Christ is not mentioned and that therefore the text is irrelevant to the point at issue. "[The] righteousness is not described as Christ's; and Paul goes on to say that it comes 'from God on the basis of faith,' so that yet again we are dealing with God's righteousness" (I, 7). But it is facile to dismiss such an important

---

[29] Hodge, *An Exposition of the Second Letter to the Corinthians*, pp. 150-151.

verse so quickly when we are dealing with reality, not just with words.

Notice that the righteousness Paul counts on having "from God" is pursued with a longing to "be found in Christ." The righteousness that he has is his because he is "found in Christ." This use of "in Christ" is positional. *In Christ by faith* is the place where God's righteousness counts as our own. Thus "being found in Christ" is the way to "have a righteousness not my own."[30] True, this does not say explicitly that *Christ's* righteousness is imputed to us, but along with the other evidence presented here that is a natural implication of this verse.

If we have God's righteousness on the basis of faith (ἐπὶ τῇ πίστει, *epi tē pistei*) and because we are in Christ (ἐν αὐτῷ, *en autō*), is there not a reality in the Trinitarian union between the Father and the Son and in the redemptive union between the believer and Christ that closes the gap between the imputed righteousness of God and the imputed righteousness of Christ?

§4.3. The Evidence for the Imputation of Christ's Righteousness from 1 Corinthians 1:30

The reality of being "in Christ" is all-important for understanding justification. We have seen that in 2 Corinthians 5:21 we "become the righteousness of God . . . *in him*" (ἐν αὐτῷ, *en autō*), and in Philippians 3:9 we "have" divine righteousness "in him" (ἐν αὐτῷ, *en autō*). Paul says explicitly in Galatians 2:17 that we are "justified *in Christ*" (δικαιωθῆναι ἐν Χριστῷ, *dikaiōthēnai en Christō*). The implication seems to be that our union with Christ

---

[30] Calvin draws the connection between our righteousness in justification and our union with Christ:

> Therefore, that joining together of Head and members, that indwelling of Christ in our heart—in short, that mystical union—are accorded by us the highest degree of importance, so that Christ, having been made ours, makes us sharers with him in the gifts with which he has been endowed. We do not, therefore, contemplate him outside ourselves from afar in order that his righteousness may be imputed to us but because we put on Christ and are engrafted into his body—in short, because he deigns to make us one with him. For this reason, we glory that we have fellowship of righteousness with him. John Calvin, *Institutes of the Christian Religion*, ed. John T. McNeill, trans. Ford Lewis Battles (Philadelphia, PA: Westminster, 1960), 3:11:10.

I am indebted to Richard Gaffin for drawing this passage to my attention.

is what connects us with divine righteousness. This truth raises the importance of 1 Corinthians 1:30.

Paul says in 1 Corinthians 1:30, "By [God's] doing you are in Christ Jesus (ἐξ αὐτοῦ δὲ ὑμεῖς ἐστε ἐν Χριστῷ ᾽Ιησοῦ, *ex autou de humeis este en Christō Iēsou*), who became to us wisdom from God, and righteousness, and sanctification, and redemption." Here is a clear statement that Christ "became for us righteousness (ἐγενήθη . . . ἡμῖν . . . δικαιοσύνη, *egenēthē . . . hēmin . . . dikaiosunē*)." Gundry again dismisses the verse as irrelevant for this issue with the words:

> That the wisdom comes from God favors that righteousness, sanctification, and redemption—which make up or parallel wisdom— likewise come from God. Thus, the righteousness that Christ becomes for us who are in him is not his own righteousness, but God's. Nor does Paul use the language of imputation. (I, 7)

This is remarkable. The text says "Christ became for us . . . righteousness," but Gundry says, "The righteousness that Christ becomes for us . . . is not his own." How can he jump so quickly to this conclusion just because the righteousness is "from God" (ἀπὸ θεοῦ, *apo theou*), especially when the verb "become" is surely as crucial as the phrase "from God"? In some sense Christ has become our righteousness. Add to this that he becomes righteousness "for us" (ἡμῖν, *hēmin*) by virtue of our being in him (ἐν Χριστῷ ᾽Ιησοῦ, *en Christō Iēsou*). And then add to that how Paul says explicitly in Galatians 2:17 that "justification" is "in Christ." This surely suggests strongly that Christ's "becoming" or "being" (as the verb ἐγενήθη [*egenēthē*] can mean) righteousness for us is related to justification—our being declared righteous.

C. K. Barrett is not as quick to dismiss this verse as Gundry is. He argues:

> The root of the thought is forensic: man is arraigned in God's court, and is unable to satisfy the judge unless righteousness,

which he cannot himself produce, is given to him. . . . Christ himself becomes righteousness for him (2 Cor. 5:21), and God the judge views him not as he is in himself but in Christ.[31]

One may object that Christ's becoming sanctification for us is not an imputed reality but rather is worked in us; so why should we assume that Christ's becoming righteousness for us refers to an imputed righteousness? In answer, I don't *assume* it. Instead I note that the other passages that connect righteousness with being "in Christ" have to do with justification (Galatians 2:17) and speak of a righteousness that is "not our own" (Philippians 3:9) and that "we become the righteousness of God" in the same way Christ became sin, that is, by imputation (2 Corinthians 5:21). Then I observe that there is no reason to think that Christ must "become" for us righteousness exactly the same way he becomes wisdom and sanctification and redemption. This is not said or implied.[32]

In fact, it is plausible to see a natural progression in the four realities that Christ is for us. In our union with Christ he becomes "wisdom" for us in overcoming the blinding and deadening *ignorance* that keeps us from seeing the glory of the cross (1 Corinthians 1:24). Then he becomes righteousness for us in overcoming our *guilt and condemnation* (Romans 8:1). Then he becomes sanctification for us in overcoming our *corruption and pollution* (1 Corinthians 1:2; Ephesians 2:10). Finally, he becomes redemption for us in overcoming, in the resurrection, all *the miseries, pain, futility, and death* of this age (Romans 8:23).[33] There is no reason to force this text to mean that Christ becomes all these

---

[31] C. K. Barrett, *A Commentary on the First Epistle to the Corinthians* (New York: Harper and Row, 1968), p. 60.

[32] This is why N. T. Wright, for example, is incorrect when he states that if we claim 1 Corinthians 1:30 as a textual basis for imputed righteousness, then "we must also be prepared to talk of the imputed wisdom of Christ; the imputed sanctification of Christ; and the imputed redemption of Christ" (N. T. Wright, *What Saint Paul Really Said* [Grand Rapids, MI: William B. Eerdmans, 1997], p. 123).

[33] I have leaned here on John Flavel from his sermon on 1 Corinthians 1:30 in John Flavel, *The Method of Grace* (Grand Rapids, MI: Baker Book House, 1977), p. 14.

things for us in exactly the same way, namely, by imputation. He may become each of these things for us as each reality requires.

Whether Paul had this progression in mind or not, 1 Corinthians 1:30 stands as a signal pointing to the righteousness of Christ that becomes ours when we are united to him by God through faith. In connection with the other texts we have seen, it is therefore warranted to speak of his righteousness being imputed to us by faith in him.

§4.4. The Evidence for the Imputation of Christ's Righteousness from Romans 10:4

The most literal, straightforward translation of Romans 10:4 would be: "For the end (or goal or consummation) of the law [is] Christ for righteousness to everyone who believes" (τέλος γὰρ νόμου Χριστὸς εἰς δικαιοσύνην παντὶ τῷ πιστεύοντι, *telos gar nomou Christos eis dikaiosunēn panti tō pisteuonti*). "Christ for righteousness" to all believers fits well with the concept of Christ's becoming our righteousness in 1 Corinthians 1:30 and points again toward Christ's righteousness as what is imputed to believers for justification.

This truth about "Christ for righteousness" in verse 4 is given as the ground or explanation (γάρ, *gar*) of verse 3 which says, "For being ignorant of God's righteousness and seeking to establish their own, they did not subject themselves to the righteousness of God." In other words, striving to establish one's own righteousness and not submitting to God's righteousness is owing to a failure to embrace the truth that "the goal of the law is Christ for righteousness to everyone who believes." Clearly then there is a close connection between "God's righteousness" and "Christ for righteousness." That connection is clarified when we look further back into the preceding context.

> *(9:30) What shall we say then? That Gentiles, who did not pursue righteousness, attained righteousness, even the righteousness which is by faith; (31) but Israel, pursuing a law of*

righteousness, did not arrive at the law. (32) Why? Because they did not pursue it by faith, but as though it were by works. They stumbled over the stumbling stone, (33) just as it is written, "Behold, I lay in Zion a stone of stumbling and a rock of offense, and he who believes in him will not be disappointed." (10:1) Brethren, my heart's desire and my prayer to God for them is for their salvation. (2) For I testify about them that they have a zeal for God, but not in accordance with knowledge. (3) For being ignorant of God's righteousness and seeking to establish their own, they did not subject themselves to the righteousness of God. (4) For the goal (or end) of the law is Christ for righteousness to everyone who believes.

Twice in Romans 9:30-32 Paul refers to "pursuing" righteousness. Gentiles, Paul says, were *not* pursuing it, but attained it. Israel *was* pursing it through the law by works and did not attain it. This "*pursuing*" is probably the same as the "*seeking*" in 10:3. Israel did not "attain or arrive at" (κατέλαβεν, *katelaben*, 9:30; ἔφθασεν, *ephthasen*, 9:31) righteousness because they were "*seeking* to establish their own" (10:3).

Two explanations are given of this failure, one in 9:32 and one in 10:4. They are probably two ways of saying the same thing. Romans 9:32 explains that Israel failed because they misused the law to "work" their way into righteousness; that is, they "stumbled over the stumbling stone," Christ. Romans 10:4 explains that Israel failed because, in trying to establish their own righteousness, they missed the aim or end of the law, namely, "Christ for righteousness." So in both explanations the failure to attain righteousness is a failure to see Christ for what he was meant to be, namely, righteousness. They stumbled over him, that is, they rejected him, because they did not recognize that the goal of the law was that Christ be (or provide) their righteousness. "The goal (or end) of the law is *Christ for righteousness* for everyone who believes" (10:4).

How is one to avoid this failure to "attain" or "arrive at"

righteousness? By having faith in Christ.[34] "Gentiles . . . attained
. . . a righteousness that is *by faith*" (9:30). Israel failed to attain
righteousness because they did not pursue it "by faith." The
opposite of stumbling over "the rock of offense" is to "believe in
him" (9:33). This is why "Christ for righteousness" in 10:4 is
said to be "for everyone who believes." He becomes righteousness for us when we believe on him.

Therefore, the flow of thought from Romans 9:30 to 10:4
leads us to believe that the framework of ideas is the same as
we have been seeing in 2 Corinthians 5:21, Philippians 3:9, and
1 Corinthians 1:30. Sinners need *righteousness* to stand before
God. That is why it is being "pursued" by Israel. That much they
got right. But whose righteousness will suffice? The declaration
of righteousness before God, called justification, does not rest on
a fiction.[35] There is real righteousness as the basis of it. But as sinners we will never be able to provide "our *own* righteousness"
(Philippians 3:9; Romans 10:3). We must "attain" righteousness
another way besides doing good works. No good works of any
kind will make a fallen person righteous before God.[36] The way

---

[34] Paul is not addressing in Romans 9:30–10:4 the issue of Israel's faith apart from Christ; he is dealing with the crisis that Christ's coming created for Israel. He was a rock of offense. The failure spoken of in 9:30-31 is not a general failure in the Old Testament, but the spe- cific failure to trust Christ when he came. They stumbled over him. They failed to see in him the goal of the law, "Christ for righteousness."

[35] J. I. Packer writes: "[God] reckons righteousness to them, not because he accounts them to have kept his law personally (which would be a false judgment), but because he accounts them to be united to one who kept it representatively (and that is a true judgment)" (J. I. Packer, "Justification," in *Evangelical Dictionary of Theology*, ed. Walter A. Elwell [Grand Rapids, MI: Baker, 1984], p. 596).

[36] Paul is able to speak of "works" (ἔργων, *ergōn*) in both a positive and negative sense. For example, the "works of the law" (ἔργων νόμου, *ergōn nomou*) are always spoken of dis- paragingly in connection with justification (Romans 3:20, 28; Galatians 2:16; 3:2, 5, 10); and yet Paul can write about the necessity of good works that are caused by faith (e.g., 2 Corinthians 9:8; Ephesians 2:10; Colossians 1:10; 1 Thessalonians 1:3; 2 Thessalonians 1:11; 1 Timothy 5:25; 6:18; 2 Timothy 2:21; 3:17; Titus 2:7, 14; 3:1, 8, 14). It is a mistake to argue, however, that in distinguishing these two types of "works" Paul thinks that the good form of works is instrumental in our justification. Paul argues that no works of any kind are involved in the means of justification. Ephesians 2:8-10 says that we are not saved through works, including the works that God prepared beforehand for us to walk in. There is a great deal of overlap in Romans 3 and 4 between "works" and "works of the law," such that the latter is a subset of the former. No works—either done in accordance with the Mosaic Law or done by faith—can be the means of justifying the ungodly. See Douglas J. Moo, "'Law,' 'Works of the Law,' and Legalism in Paul," *Westminster Theological Journal* 45 (1983): 73-100.

appointed by God is "by faith," and what faith does is connect us to "Christ for righteousness." Christ "became to us righteousness." In him we "have" a righteousness from God based on faith (Philippians 3:9). In him we become the righteousness of God (2 Corinthians 5:21).

If one allows for biblical reflection and comparison and synthesis and a desire to penetrate to reality behind words (as with, for example, the biblical doctrines of the Trinity, the two natures of Christ, or the substitutionary atonement), then the doctrine of the imputation of Christ's righteousness is not an artificial construct of systematic theologians but is demanded by the relevant texts.

§4.5. The Evidence for the Imputation of Christ's Righteousness from Romans 5:12-19

One of the most crucial texts for the traditional Protestant teaching that Christ's righteousness and obedience are the expression of God's righteousness that is imputed to us by faith is Romans 5:12-19. This passage brings Paul's exposition of justification in Romans 3—5 to a climax with a stunning comparison between the effect of Adam's disobedience on those who are in him and the effect of Christ's obedience on those who are in him.

§4.5.1. THE INCOMPLETE SENTENCE OF ROMANS 5:12

Paul begins his comparison between Adam and Christ with the words "just as." "Therefore, *just as* through one man sin entered into the world, and death through sin, and so death spread to all men, because all sinned . . ." Then Paul breaks off. We expect the clause introduced by "just as" to be followed by a clause introduced by "so also": "*Just as* through one man sin entered into the world . . . *so also* through one man righteousness entered the world . . ." or something like that. In fact he will pick up the comparison in verse 18 ("*As* one trespass led to condemnation for all men, *so* one act of righteousness leads to justification and life for all men"). But here he breaks off and doesn't complete it. Why?

Probably because he realizes that he has just said something that is liable to be misunderstood and needs to be clarified. What was that? Several things, but he picks out one in particular, because if he can make this one clear, it will keep the others from being misunderstood. He wants to clarify what he means at the end of verse 12 by the phrase, "for all sinned." This is just where he breaks off. "Just as through one man sin entered into the world, and death through sin, and so death spread to all men, *because all sinned . . .*"

First he says that through one man, Adam, sin entered the world, and through sin, death—the judgment on sin. Then he broadens out this statement and says that this death, this judgment, was not confined to one man but spread to all humans. Why? Here comes the ambiguity. He says, "Because all sinned." Does this mean "because all sinned in Adam"? Was Adam's sin imputed to us, so that we are viewed as sinning in him? Or does it mean that the penalty and judgment of death is owing to our moral corruption and individual acts of sin and not to Adam's sin being imputed to us?[37] I think the context urges us to conclude that we all sinned in Adam, that his sin is imputed to us, and that universal human death and condemnation is God's judgment and penalty on all of us because we were in some deep and mysterious way united to Adam in his sinning.[38]

---

[37] Some scholars (e.g., Thomas Schreiner and Joseph Fitzmyer) reject the traditional translation "because all sinned" and argue that the phrase ἐφ' ᾧ πάντες ἥμαρτον (*eph hō pantes hēmarton*) should be rendered, "on the basis of this death all sinned." Death is understood to be the spiritual condemnation that causes sin, rather than death being the penalty of sin. (See the discussion and relevant literature in Schreiner, *Romans*, pp. 271ff.) I do not find this compelling for several reasons. 1) This would mean that in verse 12 there is a shift from death entering the world "through sin" to sin being the result of death. This seems unlikely. The idea that first sin brings about death and then death brings about sin is possible but would be surprising. 2) The connection, "sin is not counted where there is no law, but death reigned from Adam to Moses" (5:13-14), suggests that the reign of death prevails in spite of its apparent cause (sin) not being counted. Thus sin is the cause of death in Paul's thinking here, not vice versa. 3) The parallel in 5:21 points (*in this very connection*, cf. "reign") to sin as the cause of death, not death as the cause of sin. "As sin reigned in death, even so grace would reign through righteousness to eternal life through Jesus Christ our Lord." Notice that as grace reigns "to eternal life," so also sin reigns in death—that is, it leads to death.

Why does this matter? Does not Romans 3:23 teach that all have sinned and fall short of the glory of God individually? Gundry sees the parallel between this text and Romans 5:12 and believes that the sinning referred to in Romans 5:12 is not our sinning in Adam, or Adam's sin being imputed to us, but our own personal sinning for which we die (I, 8). So if our judgment and condemnation is the result of the sins we do every day (which is true), why does it matter if we find a deeper cause of our guilt and death and condemnation—namely, our union with Adam in his sinning at the beginning?

It is precisely the answer to this question, I suggest, that made Paul break off his comparison in verse 12 so that he could clarify what he meant by "because all sinned." What's at stake here is the whole comparison between Christ and Adam. If we understand "because all sinned" as "because all sinned in Adam," the entire comparison between Christ and Adam illumines the freedom and greatness of justification by grace through faith in a powerful and unique way.

Paul saw what was at stake in misunderstanding what he had said. Here is what I think Paul saw as the possible misunderstanding: If you say, "Through Adam sin and death entered the world, and death spread to everybody *because all sinned individually*," then the comparison with the work of Jesus (which is where he is heading;[39] cf. "just as . . .") would probably be, "So also, through Jesus Christ, righteousness and life entered the world, and life spread to all *because all individually did acts of righteousness*." In other words, justification would *not* be God's

---

[38] For a powerful book-length argument that Adam's sin is imputed to all humans, see John Murray, *The Imputation of Adam's Sin* (Phillipsburg, NJ: Presbyterian & Reformed, 1992; orig., 1959). For a helpful effort to think through how our union with Adam in his sin can be conceived and understood, see Jonathan Edwards, *Original Sin, The Works of Jonathan Edwards*, Vol. 3, ed. Clyde A. Holbrook (New Haven, CT: Yale University Press, 1970), pp. 389-412 (Part IV, Chapter III).

[39] "The apostle has been speaking of Adam and the damage he did in order to be able to present the effect of the act of salvation against this background." Ernst Käsemann, *Commentary on Romans*, trans. Geoffrey W. Bromiley (Grand Rapids, MI: William B. Eerdmans, 1980), p. 151.

imputing righteousness to us, but our doing individual acts of righteousness with Christ's help, which would then be counted as our righteousness. This would turn the whole point of Romans 1—5 on its head. When Paul saw *that* as a possible misunderstanding of what he said, he stopped to clarify.

Stating it positively, what would Paul be saying about the work of Christ if the words "because all sinned" actually meant "because all sinned in Adam" (not because they sinned individually)? If he meant this, the comparison with Adam would go like this:

> "*Just as* through one man sin entered the world
> > (and death through sin)
> > > and sin spread to all who are in Adam,
> > > > because all sinned in Adam
> > > > > and his sin was imputed to them,
> *so also* through one man, Jesus Christ, righteousness entered the world
> > (and life through righteousness)
> > > and life spread to all who are in Christ
> > > > because all were righteous in him
> > > > > and his righteousness is imputed to
> > > > > > them."

That, I believe, is the glory of justification by grace through faith that Paul wants us to see in this text. The basis of our justification before God is a divine righteousness that comes to us in a way analogous to the way Adam's sin came to us. As we were in him and share in his sin, so we are in Christ and share in his righteousness.

In this historic way of understanding the text, the parallel that Paul wants us to see and rejoice in is that just as Adam's sin is imputed to us because we were in him, so Christ's righteousness is imputed to us because we are in him. But is that what he really means in this passage? A key part of the answer will hang on what Paul means by "for all sinned" at the end of verse 12 and why Paul broke off his comparison. How then does he clarify his point by breaking off and inserting verses 13-14?

§4.5.2. THE CLARIFICATION OF "ALL SINNED" (VERSE 12) IN ROMANS 5:13-14

In Romans 5:13-14 Paul says, "For until the Law [of Moses], sin was in the world, but sin is not imputed when there is no law. (14) Nevertheless death reigned from Adam until Moses . . ." He is saying: 1) Sin was in the world before the Mosaic Law (v. 13a); he concedes that personal sin was prevalent in the world before Moses, not just Adam's sin. 2) But sin is not imputed (not counted, not punished) where there is no law (v. 13b). 3) "Nevertheless death reigned from Adam until Moses" (v. 14a). That is, virtually everybody died. Everybody bore the consequences of sin.

Now what is the implication that Paul wants us to see? He wants us to see that universal human death was *not* owing to individual sins against the Mosaic Law, but to man's sinning in Adam. That is what he is trying to clarify. Verse 12, at the end, says that death spread to all "because all sinned." So Paul argues and clarifies: But people died even though their own individual lawbreaking was not the reason for dying ; their individual sins weren't counted. The reason all died is because all sinned in Adam. Adam's sin was imputed to them.

§4.5.2.1 How Paul Deals with Possible Objections

But there is an objection at this point to Paul's argument, and Paul can see it coming. The objection is that even before the Mosaic Law, there were commands of God to Noah and Abraham and others. So maybe their deaths were only owing to disobeying *those* laws, not because they sinned in Adam. And not only that, the objection would go, Paul himself said back in Romans 1:32 that all people—even Gentiles outside Israel—"know the ordinance of God, that those who practice such things are worthy of death." So there seem to be two exceptions to Paul's argument: yes, there was no Mosaic Law to sin against before Moses, but 1) there were individual divine commands given before Moses (e.g., Genesis 6:13-14; 8:16-17; 17:10; 20:7; 31:13; etc.); and 2) there was the law written on the heart (Romans 2:15). So, has Paul really succeeded in showing that the people between Adam and Moses died for sinning in Adam and not for their own individual sins against these laws?

I suggested that Paul sees this objection coming, and that's why he adds the next words in verse 14. He doesn't stop by saying, "Nevertheless death reigned from Adam until Moses . . ." He goes on to add the very crucial words, "[Death reigned] even over those who had not sinned in the likeness of the offense of Adam." In other words, yes, he concedes that there were other kinds of laws before the Mosaic Law, and yes, people broke those laws, and yes, one *could* argue that these sins are the root cause of death and condemnation in the world. But, he says, there is a problem with that view, because death reigned "*even* over those who had not sinned in the likeness of the offense of Adam." There are those who died without seeing or knowing any divine law and choosing to sin against it.[40]

Who are they? I am still inclined to think, against the most common scholarly opinion, that the group of people begging for

---

[40] Moo says that "'those who did not sin in the likeness of Adam's transgression' might be a different group than those who lived between Adam and Moses. But it is more likely that the clause is a further identification of those who lived during this time period. With this description, Paul brings out the characteristic of these people that is essential to his argument: the 'law-less' context of their sin. They lived before God gave specific commandments to the people and they could not then, sin, as Adam did, by 'transgressing.'" Moo, *The Epistle to the Romans*, p. 333. I wonder if Moo is sufficiently careful here to deal with the problem that there are many commandments that God gave between Adam and Moses and that Paul conceded that even those outside the scope of special revelation "know God's decree, that those who practice such things deserve to die" (Rom. 1:32). This is why I incline to say (with Murray, *Romans,* Vol. 1, p. 190) that the "even over" (καὶ ἐπί, *kai epi*) at the beginning of verse 14 ("even over those whose sinning was not like the transgression of Adam") introduces a smaller group than all who lived between Adam and Moses.

an explanation, and providing the most relevant illustration for
Paul's point, is infants. Infants died. They could not understand
personal revelation—external or internal. They could not read
the law on their hearts and choose to obey or disobey it. Yet they
died. Why? Paul's answer in the context would be: the sin of
Adam and the imputation of that sin to the human race. In other
words, death reigned over all humans, even over those who did
not sin against a known and understood law. Therefore, the conclusion is, to use the words of verse 18: "Through one transgression there resulted condemnation to all men."

I know that many commentators object to the reference to
children. It is indeed a very difficult and complex connection of
thoughts. I do not believe my entire case hangs on this one point.
Paul's argument remains the same whether or not we are able to
specify the identity of those who "had not sinned in the likeness
of the offense of Adam." For whether or not we can identify
those whom Paul has in mind, we still have to reckon with the
fact that he tells us that there are people who died without sinning in the way Adam did. So no matter whom Paul exactly has
in mind, his point is: Personal, individual sin cannot be the reason all die, because some died without transgressing a known law
in the way Adam did (v. 14), and thus without the ability to have
their personal sins reckoned to them in the sense of which he is
speaking (v. 13). Therefore, they must have died because of the
sin of Adam imputed to them. "All sinned" in 5:12b thus means
that all sinned "through the one man's disobedience" (5:19).[41]

As I've said, my case does not hang on whether or not Paul
has infants in view. But I will try to defend it contextually. One
objection to the reference to children is that children die in *all*

---

[41] Cf. the similar observation from John Murray: "Verse 12 tells us the reason why death
passed on to all men. It is that 'all sinned.' But verse 14 tells us that death reigned over those
who did not sin after the similitude of Adam's transgression. The reign of death in verse 14
must have the same import as the passing on of death in verse 12. Hence Paul is saying that
death passed on to and reigned over those who did not personally and voluntarily transgress
as Adam did, and therefore the 'all sinned' of verse 12 cannot refer to individual personal
transgression" (Murray, *The Imputation of Adam's Sin*, pp. 20-21).

periods of history;[42] so why would Paul draw attention to the period between Adam and Moses if his argument is based on the death of children who did not sin after the likeness of Adam's transgression? My answer is that Paul was drawn to this period of history because his argument emerges in two stages, one general and loose, based on the period between Adam and Moses, the other specific and strict based on a group within that period (but also other periods).

Consider two reasons why Paul chose to focus on the period between Adam and Moses.

§4.5.2.1.1. First, what Paul had in mind as he said, "Death spread to all men, because all sinned" was probably the general principle he laid down in Romans 4:15 ("where there is no law there is no *transgression*," παράβασις, *parabasis*). He expresses it here in Romans 5:13, "Sin is not counted where there is no law." That principle, together with the reference to Adam's "*transgression*" (Romans 5:14, παραβάσεως, *parabaseōs*) suited his purposes almost perfectly, since it implied that, *generally speaking*, the absence of particular laws would mean the absence of particular transgressions, which would mean the absence of the death penalty. "Yet" (verse 14, ἀλλά, *alla*) people died between Adam and Moses, which pointed, *in general and loosely*, to the solidarity with Adam in his *transgression* as the cause of everyone's death, not to their own transgressions. That is one reason why Paul referred to the period between Adam and Moses.

§4.5.2.1.2. A second reason relates to the legal implications of people dying as punishment in a time period without explicit laws with explicit death penalties. In the garden God had said to Adam, "You shall not eat, for in the day that you eat of it you shall surely die" (Genesis 2:17, ESV). Here was an explicit regulation attached to an explicit death penalty. Similarly in the Law

---

[42] For example, Thomas Schreiner, *Romans:* "[Paul's] concern was not to explain the situation of those who die in infancy (since this has occurred through history) . . ." p. 277.

of Moses we read, at the outset, this typical regulation and legal sanction: "Take care not to go up into the mountain or touch the edge of it. Whoever touches the mountain shall be put to death" (Exodus 19:12, ESV). In cases like these the death penalty is more manifestly just because it is explicitly attached to the regulation. That was not the case during the time period between Adam and Moses.

The reason this observation is so relevant is that the cause of death in Paul's argument in this entire passage is primarily a *legal* issue, not a *natural* or *moral* one. What I mean is that death is not viewed here as the "natural" consequence of "moral corruption," but as the *legal* consequence of lawbreaking, that is, as "condemnation" (κατάκριμα, *katakrima*, cf. Romans 5:16, 18). We see this as the argument develops and climaxes. And that development and climax illuminate why Paul chose to set up the parallel between Adam and Christ the way he did, and why he chose to show the reign of death in a "law-less" period of history.

For example, the climax of his argument in Romans 5:20-21 returns to the very issue of 5:13-14—namely, the coming in of the written, explicit *law* where there had been none: "Now the law came in to increase the trespass, but where sin increased, grace abounded all the more, (21) so that, as sin reigned in death, grace also might reign through righteousness unto eternal life through Jesus Christ our Lord." Paul is contrasting (as in the entire passage) the triumph of "the *grace* of that one man Christ Jesus" (5:15) with the apparent triumph of sin in death. He says that this grace (vv. 15, 17, 20, 21) reigns through righteousness unto life. He does *not* mean, in this verse, that grace is a power that makes us morally righteous and brings us through moral transformation to eternal life (which is theologically true, but not the point here). Rather he means that grace brings the "gift of righteousness" (v. 17)—Christ's righteousness—which leads to "justification of life" (5:18, δικαίωσιν ζωῆς, *dikaiōsin zōēs*).

We can know this, first, because the counterpart to the "free gift" of righteousness is "judgment" (not moral corruption) in verse 16 ("the *judgment* [κρίμα, *krima*] following one trespass brought condemnation, but the *free gift* following many trespasses brought justification"). In verse 21 grace reigns "through righteousness" in the sense that the gift of righteousness triumphs over our guilt and gives us a right standing with God, which leads to life.

Second, we can know it also because the objection to 5:21 that follows in Romans 6:1 ("Are we to continue in sin that grace may abound?") would make no sense if Paul had just taught that grace was triumphant in the sense of overcoming the moral power of sin. If Paul had just said, "Grace overcomes the power of sin," the objector would not say, "Well, then, it surely looks like grace would be magnified if we yield to the power of sin."

What this means then is that Paul is primarily concerned in Romans 5:12-21 to show the *legal*, not the moral, triumph of grace over the *legal*, not the moral, problem of sin. We can see this clearly in verse 16, quoted two paragraphs back, where the problem being addressed is not the effect of Adam's sin as *corruption* with the *natural* consequence of death, but rather the effect of Adam's sin as *"condemnation"* (κατάκριμα, *katakrima*) with the *legal* consequence of death. Similarly in verse 18 the focus is not on corruption and its natural consequence, but rather on the *legal* judgment of "condemnation" ("As one trespass led to *condemnation* for all men, so one act of righteousness leads to justification and life for all men").

My point is that in Romans 5:13-14 Paul introduced the Adam-to-Moses time period because of the *legal* problem it created—namely, that the sentence of death was falling on all people, even though there was no explicit law with an attached death penalty as there was in Genesis 2:17 and Exodus 19:12.[43] I am still answering the objection that if Paul has children in view in verse 14 ("even over those whose sinning was not like the transgression of Adam"), then it makes no sense for him to have appealed first to the Adam-to-Moses time period. I have tried to give two reasons why that period is relevant.

But now I still think Paul wants to go further than that and make his point more specific and strict. He wants to cover any possible loopholes by referring to a particular group in the population between Adam and Moses, namely, "those whose sinning was not like the transgression of Adam." This is the group that I am suggesting consists at least largely of infants. So the point is *not* that Paul chose the period from Adam to Moses because children died then, but that he had other reasons for choosing that period, and then he made his argument specific and strict by adding this group.

And so, it seems to me, his point is made: At the end of verse 12 the words, "death spread to all men, because all sinned" mean that "death spread to all because all sinned *in Adam*." "The judgment following one trespass brought condemnation" for all men. Death is not first, and most deeply, owing to our own individual sinning, but to our being connected with Adam in such a way that his sin really made us guilty and liable to condemnation.[44]

---

[43] It may be—though I cannot explain it yet—that this legal issue in the time between Adam and Moses, if understood the way Paul does, would remove the entire need to postulate children as the ones he is speaking about in the words, "even over those whose sinning was not like the transgression of Adam" in Romans 5:14. It may be that the Gentiles, outside the scope of special revelation, were in a position so cut off from law and the legal sanction of a death penalty that they could not, in Paul's mind, legally be put to death ("condemnation," κατάκριμα, *katakrima*) since they had no access to an explicit law from God with the legal sanction of a death penalty. Thus they would constitute the group referred to in the words, "even over those whose sinning was not like the transgression of Adam." If this is the case, there would have to be a way to account for why Romans 1:32 does not contradict it. There Paul says that these Gentiles "know God's decree (τὸ δικαίωμα, *to dikaiōma*), that those who practice such things deserve to die (ἄξιοι θανάτου εἰσίν *axioi thanatou eisin*). So it seems that there is some kind of "death sentence" that they are aware of. But I admit that Paul may have thought about these people in a way that I do not yet understand.

[44] Gundry has a very different way of construing Romans 5:12-14. He argues that "'all have sinned' in Romans 5:12 does not mean God imputed Adam's original sin to the rest of the human race" (I, 8). Concerning the people who committed their sins "before the law was given," and "not after the likeness of Adam's transgression," he says that the way their sin-

§4.5.2.2 Why Did Paul Introduce the Adam-Christ Connection at This Place?

Now here is the all-important question: Why did Paul exactly at this place—at the end of verse 14, right after saying that death came to those who did not sin personally against an explicit law with a death penalty the way Adam did—why exactly here did Paul insert the all-important words, "who was a type of him who was to come"? Why, precisely at this point, did Paul say that Adam is a type of Christ?

He says that Adam is a type or pattern[45] of Christ because the all-important parallel is seen here. The parallel here is this: The judicial consequences of Adam's sin are experienced by all his people not on the basis of their doing sins like he did, but on the basis of their being in him and his sin being imputed to them. As soon as that becomes clear in Paul's argument—just at this point—he brings in Christ as the parallel. The point is to make clear what the focus of the parallel is: The judicial consequences of Christ's righteousness are experienced by all his people not on the basis of their doing righteous deeds like he did, but on the

---

ning was distinct from Adam's original sin is that "they did not consist of transgressions, which could be entered as debits on an account, but consisted of slave-service to sin as a dominating force" (I, 8). This strikes me as foreign to the flow of thought and the context. Paul will have much to say about slavery to sin in chapter 6, but to see this here seems unwarranted. Moreover, it does not seem to fit the thought of verse 14. When Paul says, "Death reigned from Adam to Moses, even over those whose sinning was not like the transgression of Adam," he implied that the unlikeness between their sinning and Adam's sinning made it surprising that they were dying. But Gundry's description of them as committing their sins as slave-service to a dominating force does not make it surprising that they died. Why wouldn't someone who gives himself as a slave to sin die? In fact, Paul says in Romans 6:16, "Do you not know that if you present yourselves to anyone as obedient slaves, you are slaves of the one whom you obey, either of sin, which leads to death, or of obedience, which leads to righteousness?" Gundry might say, "That's the whole point, namely, their slavery to sin, not the imputation of Adam's sin." But this does not fit the flow of thought in verse 14. Paul says that death reigned over all people before the law was given, "even over those" whose sins were not like Adam's. This "even" (or "and") implies that the group in view is different from the mass of people. They are a special and peculiar class of sinners, not all sinners before Moses. But in Gundry's view this demand of verse 14 is not apparently honored. In his view everyone between Adam and Moses is the slave of sin. So who then are those introduced by the words, "[death reigned] even over those . . ."? So I do not find Gundry's conclusion compelling when he rejects the imputation of Adam's sin as the explanation of the death of this group.

[45] "A type is a biblical event, person, or institution which serves as an example or pattern for other events, persons or institutions . . ." David L. Baker, *Two Testaments, One Bible: A Study of the Theological Relationship Between the Old and New Testaments,* revised edition (Downers Grove, IL: InterVarsity Press, 1991), p. 195.

basis of their being in him and his righteousness being imputed
to them.

That is the all-important parallel. The deepest reason why
death reigns over all is not because of our individual sins, but
because Adam's sin is imputed to us. It is "ours" by virtue of cor-
porate union with him ("in Adam all die," 1 Corinthians 15:22).
So the deepest reason why eternal life reigns is not because of our
individual deeds of righteousness,[46] but because Christ's righteousness is imputed to us by grace through faith.

The point of the comparison with Adam is to show that there
is one fundamental problem in the human race, which began
with Adam at the beginning: sin. And the burden of this text,
expressed repeatedly, is that the problem with humanity is not
most deeply our individual sinning, which might necessitate individual remedies, but rather the deadly connection that we all
have with Adam.

> *Verse 15: "By the transgression of the one [Adam] the many died."*

> *Verse 16: "The judgment followed one sin and brought con-*
> *demnation."*

> *Verse 17: "By the transgression of the one, death reigned*
> *through the one."*

> *Verse 18: "Through one transgression there resulted condem-*
> *nation to all men."*

> *Verse 19: "Through the one man's disobedience the many were*
> *appointed sinners."*

So the problem with the human race is not most deeply that
everybody does various kinds of sins. Those sins are real, they are

---

[46] In personal correspondence (02-04-02, quoted with permission), Gundry writes: "I hope
your readers won't infer that I believe eternal life reigns for that reason. In my view our individual deeds of righteousness provide no reason at all, not even a shallow reason, for the
reigning of eternal life."

huge, they are enough to condemn us, and they do indeed play a role in our condemnation. But the deepest problem is that behind all our depravity and all our guilt and all our sinning there is a deep mysterious connection with Adam, whose sin became our sin and whose judgment became our judgment. And the Savior from this condition and this damage is a Savior who stands in Adam's place as a kind of second Adam (or "the last Adam," 1 Corinthians 15:45). By his obedience he undoes what Adam did. By his obedience he fulfilled what Adam failed to do. In Adam all men were appointed (κατεστάθησαν, *katestathēsan*)[47] "sinners," but all who are in Christ are appointed (κατασταθή-σονται, *katastathēsontai*) "righteous" (5:19). In Adam all received condemnation; in Christ all receive justification (5:18).

§4.5.3. THE CONTRAST BETWEEN ADAM AND CHRIST IN ROMANS 5:15-17

Now in verses 15-19 Paul draws out the similarities and differences between Adam and Christ. His aim is to magnify the grace and sufficiency of the justification that comes through Christ for sinners. In Romans 5:15 he does something surprising. He contrasts Adam's "transgression" with a "free gift." He says, "But the free gift (χάρισμα, *charisma*) is not like the transgression (παράπτωμα, *paraptōma*). For if, by the transgression of the one, the many died, much more did the grace of God and the gift (δωρεα, *dōrea*) by the grace of the one Man, Jesus Christ, abound to the many" (5:15).

This is surprising because we expect him to contrast Adam's transgression with Christ's obedience or righteousness. The implication seems to be that Christ's righteousness is a *gift* that sinners may receive. This is, in fact, made explicit in verse 17 where the gift is defined as "the gift *of righteousness*" (τῆς δωρεᾶς τῆς δικαιοσύνης, *tēs dōreas tēs dikaiosunēs*). "If, because of one man's trespass, death reigned through that one

---

[47] See §4.5.4 below for a defense and explanation of this translation, including notes 51-56.

man, much more will those who receive the abundance of grace and the *free gift of righteousness* reign in life through the one man Jesus Christ" (5:17).

So Adam's transgression is contrasted with Christ's righteousness,[48] which is understood as a gift. The implication is that although Adam's transgression brought death to many, Christ's righteousness, as a free gift, abounded (ἐπερίσσευσεν, *eperisseusen*) for many. How it abounded for them is made explicit in verse 17: "Those who receive the abundance (περισσείαν, *perisseian*) of grace and the free gift of righteousness [will] reign in life through the one man Jesus Christ." In other words, the "free gift" in verse 15 is not the gift of eternal life, but the gift of righteousness that *obtains* eternal life. Thus Paul begins to develop the contrasts and similarities between Adam and Christ to magnify the superiority of Christ's righteousness over Adam's sin.

He continues this contrast in verse 16.

> *The gift (δώρημα, dōrēma) is not like what came through the one who sinned; for, on the one hand, the judgment (κρίμα, krima) arose from one transgression resulting in condemnation (κατάκριμα, katakrima), but on the other hand the free gift (χάρισμα, charisma) arose from many transgressions resulting in justification (δικαίωμα, dikaiōma).*

Notice three things from verse 16: 1) the nature of "justification"; 2) the nature of the "judgment" that leads to "condemnation"; and 3) the nature of the *foundation* for justification.

First, in verse 16 "condemnation" is the counterpart of "justification." This shows the legal, courtroom nature of justification. Justification is the opposite of condemnation; that is, it is the courtroom declaration of not guilty, or righteous. Justification is not liberation from sinning, but a declaration of

---

[48] I call the "gift of righteousness" (5:17) "Christ's righteousness" 1) because of its apparent parallel in verse 15 with Adam's trespass; and 2) because it seems to be identical with the "one act of righteousness" in verse 18, which is parallel with Christ's obedience in verse 19.

righteousness. Its opposite is not slavery to sin, but condemnation for sin.

Second, verse 16 says that there was a "judgment" that resulted in "condemnation." What was this judgment? One might answer: The judgment that results in condemnation is our fallen nature and our individual sins. But that would not fit well with verse 14 where Paul says that our condemnation—namely, death—reigned "even over those who had not sinned in the likeness of the offense of Adam." In other words, Paul wants to stress that it was *Adam's* act, not ours, that is the ultimate ground of condemnation. He makes it explicit in verse 18: "Through *one* transgression there resulted condemnation to all men."

What, then, is this judgment in verse 16 that "results in condemnation"? I think it is the counting of Adam's sin as our sin, on the basis of our union with Adam. God established a just and fitting union between Adam and his posterity, and, on the basis of that, when Adam sinned, the judgment that leads to condemnation was the reckoning of Adam's sin as belonging to all of humanity, which was united to him. That judgment, Paul says, resulted in condemnation. So our condemnation *does* have a basis in *our* sin. But it is not ours merely the way all our individual sins are ours; this "original" sin is ours on the basis of our union with Adam. It is through "one transgression"—Adam's transgression—that condemnation resulted to all (verse 18).

Third, notice, in the last half of verse 16, that the "free gift" (which is the "gift of righteousness" according to verse 17) *results in* justification: "The free gift arose from many transgressions resulting in justification." This is crucial because it shows that there is a *foundation* for justification in "the gift of [Christ's] righteousness." We must not miss this: Justification is *not* "the free gift" in verse 16. The free gift *results in* justification." Literally, "the free gift is *unto* justification" (χάρισμα . . . εἰς δικαίωμα, *charisma . . . eis dikaiōma*). In other words, Paul is talking about the *ground or the basis* of justification in verse 16, and he is saying that it is the gift of Christ's righteousness.[49] In verse 18 Paul will call this basis of justification the "one act of righteousness," and in verse 19 he will call it "the obedience of the One." This means that we are justified—declared righteous before God—on the basis of Christ's righteousness, or Christ's obedience.

Romans 5:17 gives another reason (γάρ, *gar*) why the free gift is not *like* the effect of Adam's sin (5:16), but totally *outstrips* this one-to-one correspondence of the type and anti-type. Paul's point is that the triumph of God's grace and gift of righteousness will not simply replace the reign of death with the reign of life, but rather "much more" will make *believers reign in life* like kings in the presence of our Father forever and ever. He says, "For if by the transgression of the one, death reigned through the one, much more those who receive the abundance of grace and of the gift of righteousness will reign in life through the One, Jesus Christ." We would expect him to say, "As death reigned through the one, much more will life reign through the One." But what he says is more startling: *Life* is not pictured as reigning—*believers* are. And the basis of this reign in eternal life (5:21) is "the abundance of grace and of the gift of [Christ's] righteousness."

§4.5.4. THE CRUCIAL CONTRASTS OF ROMANS 5:18-19

Now in Romans 5:18 Paul takes us back to the comparison he began, but didn't finish, in verse 12: "Just as Adam . . . so also Christ." Paul draws out a concluding summary statement of what he has been developing in the parallels and contrasts

---

[49] Gundry observes that the "language of giving and receiving a gift, though it would be compatible with imputation, neither demands it nor equates with it" (I, 8). Then he concludes, "Moreover, the preceding verses have put in parallel Adam's one transgression and Christ's one act of righteousness, not in that both have been imputed, but in that both have occasioned the entry into the world of ruling forces: death and life-giving grace, respectively" (I, 8). Besides what I say in the body of the text, I would only observe that while gift language does not "demand" or "equate with" the language of imputation, it does fit well with it and is, I would argue, the best way to construe it.

between Adam and Christ. His aim is to clarify and magnify the greatness of the reality of justification on the basis of Christ's righteousness. So in verse 18 he says, "So then as through one transgression there resulted condemnation (κατάκριμα, *katakrima*) to all men, even so through one act of righteousness (δικαιώματος, *dikaiōmatos*)[50] there resulted justification of life (δικαίωσιν ζωῆς, *dikaiōsin zōēs*) to all[51] men."

Notice the main point about justification in verse 18: It happens to all who are connected to Christ the same way condemnation happened to those who were connected to Adam. How is that? Adam acted sinfully, and because we were connected to him, we are condemned in him. Christ acted righteously, and because we are connected to Christ we are justified in Christ. Adam's sin is counted as ours. Christ's "act of righteousness" is counted as ours.

Verse 19 supports this by saying it another way to make sure we get the main point: "For as through the one man's disobedience the many were made (κατεστάθησαν,

---

[50] For those who note that this same word is translated "justification" in verse 16, John Murray gives a helpful explanation why two different translations are fitting: "The sense in which a word is used is determined, first of all, by the immediate context. In verse 16 the sense is determined by the contrast with condemnation. But in verse 18 there is a different contrast, and this term is placed in antithesis to trespass, not to condemnation. It is this contrast that fixes the sense here." Murray, *Romans*, Vol. 1, p. 200.

[51] Who are these "all men"? Does it mean that every human being who is in Adam will also be justified so that no one will perish and that there is no such thing as eternal punishment for anyone? I don't think so, for several reasons. 1) Verse 17 speaks of "*receiving*" the gift of righteousness as though some do and some don't. Verse 17: "For if by the transgression of the one, death reigned through the one, much more *those who receive the abundance of grace and of the gift of righteousness* will reign in life through the One, Jesus Christ." That does not sound like everybody does receive it. 2) "Justification of life to all men" in Romans 5:18 does not mean all humans are justified because Paul teaches clearly in this very book and elsewhere that there is eternal punishment and all humans are not justified. For example, in Romans 2:5 he says, "But because of your stubbornness and unrepentant heart you are storing up wrath for yourself in the day of wrath and revelation of the righteous judgment of God," and then in verses 7 and 8 he contrasts this wrath with "eternal life" and so shows that it is eternal wrath, not temporary wrath. So there will be some who are not justified but come under the wrath of God forever and others who have eternal life. 3) "Justification of life to all men" in Romans 5:18 does not mean all humans are justified because in all of Romans up till now justification is not automatic as if every human receives it, but it is "by faith." Romans 5:1, "Therefore, having been *justified by faith* . . ." Romans 3:28, "For we maintain that a man is *justified by faith* apart from works of the Law." 4) A universalistic reading of Paul's "all" statements renders Paul's intense grief (Romans 9:3)—to the point of wishing he could perish, if possible, on their behalf—unintelligible.

katestathēsan) sinners, even so through the obedience of the One the many will be[52] made (κατασταθήσονται, *katastathēsontai*) righteous" (NASB). Two differences from verse 18 shed light on the meaning.

One is that Paul becomes more specific in explaining how Adam's sin brings condemnation and how Christ's righteousness brings justification. The translation "through the one man's disobedience the many *were made* sinners" and "through the obedience of the One many *will be made* righteous" is ambiguous. Does "made sinners" and "made righteous" mean that they were "counted as sinners" (in relation to Adam) and "counted as righteous" (in relation to Christ), or that they were corrupted into sinners and transformed into ethically righteous people?

Does Christ's one act of righteousness "result in justification of life" (5:18) because by this act (= the obedience of verse 19) we are transformed by faith into righteous people or because we are counted to be righteous at the moment we believe in Christ, when in fact we are ungodly (4:5)? The word translated "made"[53] (καθίστημι, *kathistēmi*) regularly means "appoint."[54] This would point to the second meaning: "through the obedience of Christ we are appointed or reckoned righteous." This would support the imputation of righteousness to us. But the word (καθίστημι, *kathistēmi*) itself may carry the implication

---

[52] The future tense here does not necessarily suggest that Paul has in view the age to come or the last judgment. It is probably simply owing to the fact that as history moves forward more and more people *will* believe and be counted righteous when they believe. The effect of Adam's sin was automatic and affected all people in the moment he sinned; hence the past tense ("many were made sinners"). The effect of Christ's obedience was not automatic and affects only those who *will* believe. This is not to deny, of course, that there is an eschatological dimension to justification in which God confirms our right standing with him, on the basis of Christ's obedience alone, with the fruit-bearing work of the Spirit as the necessary evidence and public proof that we have indeed been justified.

[53] For example, in the KJV, RSV, NIV, NASB, and ESV.

[54] For example, Matthew 24:45, 47; Luke 12:14 ("who appointed me a judge over you?"); Acts 6:3 (the first deacons were to be appointed); Acts 7:10 (God appointed Joseph ruler over Egypt); Titus 1:5 ("appoint elders in every city").

of having the qualities to which it is appointed.[55] So "the context decides."[56]

I have tried to argue that the whole context, beginning at verse 12, teaches the "imputation" of Adam's sin to the human race so as to shed light on the meaning of justification as the imputation of Christ's righteousness. The whole reason why Paul launched into this typology between Adam and Christ was to make the nature of justification (namely, as imputation) clear. The note was sounded in verses 13-14: "Until the law sin was in the world, but sin is not imputed when there is no law. Nevertheless death reigned from Adam until Moses, even over those who had not sinned in the likeness of Adam's transgression."

In other words, Paul is jealous to say that the condemnation following Adam's sin was *not* owing to our personal transgressions, but to our connection with Adam. This is so crucial to him because all the way along in this text he wants us to see that, likewise, justification does not flow from our personal obedience but from the "gift of righteousness" (5:16, 17) or the "one act of righteousness" (5:18) or "the obedience" of Christ (5:19). The whole context calls for the common meaning of καθίστημι (*kathistēmi*) in verse 19, namely, "appoint." Through the obedience of the One, many will be appointed or counted righteous.[57]

Another difference between verse 19 and verse 18 is the reference to the "obedience" of Christ rather than his "one act of righteousness." Paul's aim here seems to be to show that the nature of the righteousness we are talking about in verse 18 is

---

[55] For example, James 4:4, "Whoever wishes to be a friend of the world makes (καθίσταται, *kathistatai*) himself an enemy of God." And 2 Peter 1:8, "For if these qualities are yours and are increasing, they render (καθίστησιν, *kathistēsin*) you neither useless nor unfruitful."

[56] That is the conclusion of Albrecht Oepke on this word in *Theological Dictionary of the New Testament*, ed. Gerhard Kittel, Vol. 3 (Grand Rapids, MI: William B. Eerdmans, 1965), p. 445.

[57] Gundry says that "even if the verb [καθίστημι, *kathistēmi*] be taken to entail a forensic declaration, as some commentators do take it, Paul does not say that believing sinners are declared righteous through having Christ's obedience imputed to them" (II, 15). Yes, not in so many words, but the connection of thought does point strongly in this direction, which is the burden of my exegesis. Pointing out, as Gundry does continually, that imputation is not mentioned *explicitly* is not a compelling support for its absence *conceptually*.

compliance with the will of God and corresponds to Adam's disobedience. Adam did *not* comply with God's will, and we were counted or appointed sinners in him. Christ *did* comply with his Father's will, and we are counted righteous (obedient) in him.

Paul's point is that our righteousness before God, our justification, is not based on what we have done, but on what Christ did. His righteous act, his obedience, is counted as ours. We are counted, or appointed, righteous in him. It is a real righteousness, and it is ours, but it is ours only by imputation—or to use Paul's language from earlier in the letter, God "imputes righteousness" to us apart from works (4:6), or "righteousness is imputed" to those who believe (4:9).

§4.5.5. Does Christ's "One Act of Righteousness" Refer to His Life of Obedience?

Now what does Christ's "one act of righteousness" (5:18) and his "obedience" (v. 19) refer to? I do not think the historic doctrine of the imputation of the righteousness of Christ depends on proving that these phrases refer to the *entire life of Christ's obedience*. I do think that this is in fact what Paul means, but the really crucial and more important thing at stake in the controversy is whether *any* of Christ's "obedience" or "act(s) of righteousness" are imputed to us. In other words, does Paul teach a doctrine of justification that includes the imputation of a divine righteousness—namely, Christ's? So I am much more eager to show that the imputation of Christ's divine righteousness (as opposed to impartation) is what Paul teaches than I am to prove that Paul thought of the entire life of Jesus as included in the "act of righteousness" in Romans 5:18 (ESV).

Gundry denies that Christ's one act of righteousness is "inclusive of both his life and his death."

> That one act of righteousness does not include Jesus' previous life any more than Adam's contrastive one transgression included a

subsequent life of sinning. Contextually, Jesus' one act of righteousness refers to his dying for the ungodly, dying for us while we were still sinners, shedding his blood for our justification, and reconciling us to God through his death—period. (II, 15)

He gives several "data" in support of this view. I will mention them and give brief responses to show why I don't find them compelling.

First, Gundry calls attention to "[the references earlier in Romans 5 to Christ's] dying for the ungodly, dying for us while we were still sinners, shedding his blood for our justification, and reconciling us to God through his death [vv. 6-11]."

In other words, Christ's death has been the focus of Christ's obedience in Romans. This would only be compelling if we assumed that the atoning aspects of Christ's death provide *all* that goes into giving us a right standing with the Father. But in fact we saw above that Romans 4 develops a view of justification that encompasses more than blood-bought pardon. It encompasses the imputation of God's righteousness.[58]

Second, Gundry argues from "the absence of any contextual indication that Christ's obedience included his previous life of obedience to the law."

To this I would give four responses.

First, does not the word "obedience" in Romans 5:19 with-

---

[58] It may be helpful here to observe with Jonathan Edwards that Christ's death itself both paid the penalty for sin and accomplished our positive righteousness. This is one reason why in Scripture there is not a significant distinction made between Christ's life of obedience and Christ's death. For Christ's death is his crowning act of obedience—the culminating act of obedience to the will of God such that in it Jesus perfectly fulfills the law of God imposed upon him, such that he achieves a positive righteousness for us. Edwards says, "It is true that Christ's willingly undergoing those sufferings which he endured, is a great part of that obedience or righteousness by which we are justified. The sufferings of Christ are respected in Scripture under a twofold consideration, either merely as his being substituted for us, or put into our stead, in suffering the penalty of the law; and so his sufferings are considered as a satisfaction and propitiation for sin; or as he, in obedience to a law or command of the Father, voluntarily submitted himself to those sufferings, and actively yielded himself up to bear them; and so they are considered as his righteousness, and a part of his active obedience. Christ underwent death in obedience to the command of the Father. . . . And this is part, and indeed the principal part, of the active obedience by which we are justified." (Jonathan Edwards, *The Works of Jonathan Edwards*, Vol. 1 [Edinburgh: The Banner of Truth Trust, 1987], pp. 638-639.)

out any limitation itself provide that clue? Gundry gives the impression that it is easy and natural to picture Christ's death as a single act of obedience. But is it? Were there not many acts of obedience in Jesus' final days and hours? Are we to think of the obedience of Gethsemane, or the obedience when the mob took him away, or the obedience when he was interrogated, or the obedience when he was crowned with thorns, or the obedience when he was flogged, or the obedience when he was nailed to the cross, or the obedience when he spoke words of love to his enemies, or the obedience when he offered up his spirit to his Father? Is not Gundry treating the death of Christ as a unified act involving many acts of obedience? If so, then it seems arbitrary to draw the line at some point in the final hours or days of Jesus' life and say that the obedience before that hour was not part of the righteousness that "leads to justification" (v. 18) or part of the "obedience" that constitutes many righteous (v. 19).

Second, the word translated "act of righteousness" in verse 18, ESV (δικαιώματος, *dikaiōmatos*) is used in Romans 8:4 to refer, in the singular, to the entire scope of what the law requires: ". . . so that the requirement (δικαίωμα) of the Law might be fulfilled in us, who do not walk according to the flesh but according to the Spirit." This suggests that in Paul's mind the "one act of righteousness" that resulted in our justification may well refer to the entire obedience of Jesus viewed as a single whole—as one great act of righteousness—rather than any single act he did in life.

Third, keep in mind the parallel between verses 16 and 18. In verse 16 Paul spoke of the "free gift [of righteousness]"[59] that "brought justification." In verse 18 he speaks of "one act of righteousness resulting in justification." So we should adjust our thinking to see the righteousness and obedience of Christ as a gift. Then we should keep in mind the contextual demand that this gift

---

[59] See §4.5.3 above on Romans 5:16 and 17 for the evidence that the free gift is a gift of righteousness because of the use of that term in verse 17: δωρεᾶς τῆς δικαιοσύνης, *dōreas tēs dikaiosunēs*.

of righteousness is the positive counterpart to the sin of Adam, which was imputed to those who are in him. This shows us that it is not arbitrary or foreign to the context to see the obedience of Christ as a gift that is imputed to us, resulting in justification. In fact, I think Paul wrote this entire paragraph to make this point.

Fourth, any act of disobedience or unrighteousness in Jesus' life would have disqualified him from being our righteousness (or our substitutionary sacrifice), not just disobedience at the end of his life. In Matthew 3:15, at his baptism, Jesus said to John the Baptist, "In this way it is fitting for us to fulfill all righteousness." So from beginning to the end in his ministry Jesus was fulfilling one great "requirement of righteousness" (which is probably what δικαιώματος [dikaiōmatos] means in Romans 5:18).

Third, Gundry points out "the extremely scant attention that Paul pays elsewhere to Christ's previous life, and the extremely heavy emphasis that Paul lays elsewhere on the death of Christ."

The theological importance of the perfect life of Jesus does not depend on any extensive treatment of that life. And I have no quarrel that the death of Jesus has central stage in Paul's theology and is the climax and consummation of Christ's obedience, so that it receives greater attention.

Further, Gundry refers to "the present antithetical parallel with Adam's transgression, which hardly refers to a whole life of sinning but refers instead to the original sin in Eden."

This is not compelling because in the nature of the two cases (of Adam's disobedience and Christ's obedience) something different is called for to bring about the result. For Adam, one single sin brought condemnation immediately, so that the rest of his life was lived under that condemnation as the penalty of it. He did not have to live a life of disobedience to bring condemnation on himself and his posterity. But this is not the case with Christ's obedience. A period of obedience in Jesus' life that was followed by any act of disobedience would have disqualified Christ as the ground of our justification. Therefore the very nature of the two cases demands that Adam's disobedience be singular and Christ's obedience be cumulative.

Finally, Gundry observes "the singularizing of both Adam's transgression and Christ's act of righteousness by the modifier 'one.'"

This is not significantly different from the preceding observation, and I have given my essential answer to it there and in the answer to his second observation above. I will simply add here John Murray's answer to a similar objection:

> If the question be asked how the righteousness of Christ could be defined as "one righteous act," the answer is that the righteousness of Christ is regarded in its compact unity in parallelism with the one trespass, and there is good reason for speaking of it as the one righteous act because, as the one trespass is the trespass of the one, so that one righteousness is the righteousness of the one and the unity of the person and his accomplishment must always be assumed.[60]

I conclude then from Romans 5:12-19 that there is good exegetical warrant for seeing here a righteousness of Christ that is imputed to sinners who believe. This righteousness is the ground of their justification.

§5. THE RELATIONSHIP BETWEEN CHRIST'S "BLOOD AND RIGHTEOUSNESS"

At this point it would be helpful to address more directly the relationship between the death of Christ and the righteousness of Christ as the ground of our justification. Gundry rightly makes the death of Christ central in the act of justification, but he does this to the exclusion of the imputation of divine righteousness. Does Paul's emphasis on the death of Christ and its provision of

---

[60] Murray, *Romans,* Vol. 1, pp. 201-202.

forgiveness mean that there is no coherent place for the doctrine of imputation?

There is no question that Paul speaks of justification as "by [Christ's] *blood*" (Romans 5:9), or reconciliation as "through the *death* of [God's] Son" (Romans 5:10), or being justified as "a gift by [God's] grace through the redemption which is in Christ Jesus, whom God displayed publicly as a propitiation in his *blood* through faith" (Romans 3:24-25). All these texts relate the reality of justification to the death of Christ. Moreover, Christ's death is explicitly related to the forgiveness of our sins, for example, in Ephesians 1:7, "In him we have redemption through his blood, the forgiveness of our trespasses," or Hebrews 9:22, "without the shedding of blood there is no forgiveness."

But there are serious exegetical obstacles to keep us from emphasizing the forgiveness of sins through the death of Christ to the exclusion of the imputation of divine righteousness as an essential component of justification. Most of these we have seen so far, but one I will draw out more fully now.

§5.1. The Meaning of "Justify" (δικαιόω, dikaioō)[61]

The Greek word for "justify" (δικαιόω, *dikaioō*) does not mean "forgive." It means to declare righteous, usually in a court of law. A prisoner who is found guilty and is forgiven would not be called "justified" in the ordinary use of the word. He is justified if he is found not guilty. Forgiveness means to be found guilty and then not have the guilt reckoned to you but let go. So we should be careful that we not assume justification and forgiveness are identical.

§5.2. Texts Pointing to the Imputation of Righteousness[62]

In addition to the meaning of the word "justify," there are the texts we have discussed above that speak of God's imputing righ-

---

[61] See note 22.

[62] See Chapter Three, §§2 and 4.

teousness to us, or of our "having" a righteousness not our own (e.g., Romans 4:5, 6, 11, 24; 5:17, 18, 19; 10:4; 2 Corinthians 5:21; Philippians 3:9). The language of the imputation of righteousness in these passages cannot simply be reduced to forgiveness. For example, the words, "God credits righteousness apart from works" (Romans 4:6), or "that righteousness might be credited to them" (Romans 4:11), or "not having a righteousness of my own derived from the law, but that which is through faith in Christ, the righteousness that comes from God on the basis of faith" (Philippians 3:9)—these words mean more than not having our sins reckoned to us; they mean more than forgiveness of sins. They mean that a righteousness is credited to our account (the accounting imagery is explicit in Romans 4:4).

§5.3. Justification and Forgiveness in Relation to the Use of Psalm 32 in Romans 4

A crucial question in this regard is why Paul follows his reference to reckoning righteousness apart from works in Romans 4:6 with a reference to Psalm 32, which speaks of forgiveness. Does this mean that justification is just another way of speaking about forgiveness, and the imputation of divine righteousness is therefore superfluous? After saying in Romans 4:5 that God "justifies the ungodly," Paul then says, "Just as David also speaks of the blessing on the man to whom God credits righteousness apart from works: (7) 'Blessed are those whose iniquities are *forgiven*, and whose sins are *covered*; (8) blessed is the man against whom the Lord will *not reckon* his sin.'" Some interpreters argue that this juxtaposition of justification language (4:5, 6) and forgiveness language (4:7) means that justification is virtually synonymous with forgiveness.[63]

---

[63] For example, Daniel Fuller seems to treat the crediting image of Genesis 15:6 (used in Romans 4:3-8) as interchangeable with forgiveness. In reference to Genesis 15:6 he says, "Then comes the declaration of forgiveness in verse 6." Then he says that Romans 4:6-8 "leaves no doubt about the meaning Paul gave to the word 'credited' as he quoted Genesis 15:6: . . . Paul emphasized that Abraham was forgiven." *The Unity of the Bible: Unfolding God's Plan for Humanity* (Grand Rapids, MI: Zondervan, 1992), pp. 255-256.

But there are contextual clues that this is not the case. After quoting these two verses from Psalm 32, what Paul picks up on is not the words "forgiven" or "covered" or "not reckon," but rather on the word "blessed." This is very significant because of where he goes with it. He asks in Romans 4:9, "Is this *blessing* pronounced only upon the circumcised, or also upon the uncircumcised?" Then he does something amazing. He answers his question *not* by referring to David's situation, but by referring to Abraham; and *not* in terms of forgiveness, but in terms of faith being reckoned for righteousness. He says, "We say that faith was reckoned to *Abraham* for righteousness." Then he finishes his point with this reasoning:

> *How then was it credited? While he was circumcised, or uncircumcised? Not while circumcised, but while uncircumcised; (11) and he received the sign of circumcision, a seal of the righteousness of the faith that he had while uncircumcised. The purpose was to make him the father of all who believe without being circumcised, that righteousness might be credited to them. (Romans 4:10-11).*

Don't miss how unusual this is. Paul asks whether *David's* blessing of forgiveness was pronounced on the circumcised or on the uncircumcised, but he answers by saying that "righteousness was credited to [*Abraham*]" (v. 11) before he was circumcised. Does this not suggest strongly that the "blessing" referred to in David's words from Psalm 32 is "the crediting of righteousness" to believers, not simply the forgiveness of sins?

Now why might this be? The answer I would suggest is that Paul assumed two things: First, Paul assumes there is no justification—no positive declaration and imputation of righteousness—where there is no forgiveness. Forgiveness is a constitutive element of justification. The sins that stand in the way of declaring a person righteous must be blotted out, covered, forgiven. Second, Paul assumes that if a saving "blessing" is pronounced over a person, he must be counted as righteous. That is why he had no problem explaining David's blessing with Abraham's justification.

When Paul put Psalm 32:1-2 and Genesis 15:6 together, he saw two essential aspects of justification: forgiveness and imputation—"blotting out" and "crediting to." So when he heard David say that a forgiven person is "blessed," he heard in the "blessing" the complete work of justification without which there is no blessing—namely, the work of forgiveness *and* imputation.

This gives much help in thinking about the relationship between forgiveness and imputation in determining the ground of justification. It suggests that we should not assume justification means only forgiveness of sins. Here again 2 Corinthians 5:21 is crucial: "[God] made him who knew no sin to be sin on our behalf, so that we might become the righteousness of God in him." The first half of this verse refers to Christ's sin-bearing sacrifice for us. As Isaiah 53:5 says, "He was pierced through for our transgressions, he was crushed for our iniquities; the chastening for our well-being fell upon him." And as the apostle Peter says, "He himself bore our sins in his body on the cross" (1 Peter 2:24). "Christ also died for sins once for all, the just for the unjust" (1 Peter 3:18). This is what Paul means in the first half of 2 Corinthians 5:21: On the cross Christ "was made sin" for us.

But notice that Paul does *not* say that this leads to forgiveness (although it does), or that Christ's becoming sin for us is the *same* as justification. He says that this happened "*so that* (ἵνα, *hina*) we might become the righteousness of God in him." This result is more than forgiveness. This is our becoming righteous in Christ in a way similar to Christ's becoming sin for us. This is the other aspect of justification beyond the sin-bearing of Christ and beyond the forgiveness implicit in that sin-bearing.

Therefore, when Paul speaks of being "justified by [Christ's] blood" (Romans 5:9) we have no warrant for *equating* the totality of justification with the sin-bearing, sin-removing work of Christ or with forgiveness. But we have good warrant for saying that the death of Christ is what justifies in that 1) it provides the essential ingredient of sin removal by sacrifice so that a positive declaration will not shatter on the shoals of unforgiven sin, *and* 2) it is the climactic completion of a life of obedience (Philippians 2:8) that was essential for the imputation of righteousness to us as we are "in him" by faith (2 Corinthians 5:21). The good warrant for saying this is threefold. We are warranted 1) by the analogy of Romans 4:6-11 and 2 Corinthians 5:21, and 2) by the meaning of the word "justify" (δικαιόω, *dikaioō*), and 3) by the language of imputed righteousness in Romans 4:6, 11, 24; 10:4; Philippians 3:9.

4

CONCLUSION

Sometimes Gundry states his view with so much biblical truth that one might think his rejection of the imputation of divine righteousness is a minor tweaking of the doctrine of justification. For example, he writes,

> It is his one act of righteousness, his obedient dying of a propitiatory death, that assuaged the wrath of God so as to make God's forensic declaration of believing sinners to be righteous, both right in the upholding of divine honor and right in the fulfilling of a covenantal promise. (I, 9)

> Paul does not say that believing sinners are declared righteous through having Christ's obedience imputed to them. A forensic declaration does not equal or demand that kind of imputation. All that is needed to make forensic sense of Paul's statement [in Romans 5:19] is for Christ's obedient submission to death for our sins to result in God's declaring righteous us whose sins have thus been imputed to Christ. (II, 15)

In other words, it *appears* that Gundry holds fast to the forensic declaration of sinners as righteous as the essential meaning of justification. But then we ask Gundry, What does it mean that God "declares us righteous" if there is no doctrine of imputed divine righteousness? His answer is that "It is our faith, not Christ's righteousness, that is credited to us as righteousness" (II,

15). And the meaning he gives to this imputation of our faith as our righteousness is not that our righteousness unites us to Christ who is our righteousness, but that our righteousness consists in faith. "Since faith as distinct from works is credited as righteousness, the righteousness of faith is a righteousness that by God's reckoning *consists of faith*" (I, 8, emphasis added).

In other words, when *Christ's* righteousness is not our righteousness, it appears that something else is going to become our righteousness, and in Gundry's case it is *our own faith*. If God is going to treat us as righteous, there must be a positive ground for it besides the forgiveness for our sins.[1] Gundry seems to feel the truth of this assumption. Traditionally Protestants have said: The ground of our being declared righteous is the imputed righteousness of God, manifest in the righteousness of Christ.[2] But Gundry calls for the abandonment of this tradition and suggests (implicitly, it seems to me) that we replace the perfect righteousness of Christ with the response (by grace) of our own faith as the ground of justification.[3]

This is not good news. And I have tried to show that it is not what Paul taught. It is hard to overstate the pastoral preciousness of the truth that by faith alone, apart from[4] works (even works

---

[1] See Chapter Three, §5.1.

[2] "The righteousness of Christ on the ground of which the believer is justified is the righteousness of God. It is so designated in Scripture not only because it was provided and is accepted by him; it is not only the righteousness which avails for him before God, but it is the righteousness of the divine person; of God manifest in the flesh." Charles Hodge, *Systematic Theology*, Vol. 3 (Grand Rapids, MI: William B. Eerdmans, 1989), p. 143.

[3] This should not be meant to imply that Gundry views grace-wrought faith as the sole ground of justification. Christ's propitiatory cross-work is the ground of justification in his view. What I am arguing, however, is that Gundry implicitly sets forth another ground (a proximate ground, if you will—something that we really do [faith] that counts as our justifying righteousness) when he states that our faith is what is counted as our righteousness, while not denying Christ's propitiation as a deeper ground.

[4] The words "apart from" do not imply that the faith that unites us to Christ can be ineffectual in not giving rise to the fruit of good deeds, which Christ shed his blood to secure (Titus 2:14, "[Christ] gave himself for us to redeem us from all lawlessness and to purify for himself a people for his own possession who are zealous for good works"). True justifying faith that unites us to Christ does two things to secure our sanctification: It connects us with the power of holiness, the Holy Spirit, who bears his fruit in all the justified; and it severs the root of sin's compelling promises by cherishing Christ above all other treasures and pleasures. The phrase justification by faith alone "apart from" works simply means that the works that faith yields are not the instrument that unite us to Christ in whom we receive justification. They are the fruit of being united to Christ and the fruit of being justified by God.

done by faith),[5] we are united to Christ in whom we are counted as perfectly righteous because of his righteousness, not ours. The demand for obedience in the Christian life is undiminished and absolute. If obedience does not emerge by faith, we have no warrant to believe we are united to Christ or justified (Matthew 6:15; John 5:28-29; Romans 8:13; Galatians 6:8-9; 2 Thessalonians 2:13; James 2:17; 1 John 2:17; 3:14).

But the only hope for making progress in this radical demand for holiness and love is the hope that our righteousness before God is on another solid footing besides our own imperfect obedience as Christians. We all sense intuitively—and we are encouraged in this intuition by the demands of God—that acceptance with God requires perfect righteousness—conformity to the law (Matthew 5:48; Galatians 3:10; James 2:10). We also know that our measures of obedience, even on our best days, fall short of this standard.

The historic Protestant view of the Bible's teaching is that the basis of our hope for acceptance with God and eternal life is the provision of Christ for both pardon and perfection. That is, he becomes our substitute in two senses: In his suffering and death he becomes our curse and condemnation (Galatians 3:13; Romans 8:3); in his final suffering and death, and in his whole life of suffering and righteousness, he becomes our perfection (2 Corinthians 5:21).[6] His death is the climax of his atoning suf-

---

[5] See Chapter Three, note 35.

[6] Sometimes these two aspects of Christ's work are spoken of as his active and passive obedience. This language may sound confusing since Christ was mistreated badly and suffered during his active life, and he was very active in his obedience as he suffered the last gruesome hours of his death. But if we recognize these ambiguities, there is truth to be seen in these terms the way they have been used. For example, William Shedd writes, "By his passive righteousness is meant his expiatory sufferings, by which he satisfied the claims of justice, and by his active righteousness is meant his obedience to the law as a rule of life and conduct. It was contended by those who made this distinction, that the purpose of Christ as the vicarious substitute was to meet the entire demands of the law for the sinner. But the law requires present and perfect obedience, as well as satisfaction for past disobedience. The law is not completely fulfilled by the endurance of penalty only. It must also be obeyed. Christ both endured the penalty due to man for disobedience, and perfectly obeyed the law for him; so that he was a vicarious substitute in reference to both the precept and the penalty of the law. By his active obedience he obeyed the law, and by his passive obedience he endured the penalty. In this way his vicarious work is complete." *History of Christian Doctrine*, Vol. 2 (New York, T. & T. Clark, 1863), p. 341. John Wesley observed, "But as the active and passive righteousness of Christ were never, in fact, separated from each other, so we never need

ferings, which propitiate the wrath of God against us (Romans 3:24-25); and his death is the climax of a perfect life of righteousness—God's righteousness[7]—imputed to us (2 Corinthians 5:21; Romans 4:6, 11 with 3:21-22; 5:18-19). This meets our need for more than forgiveness, as Leon Morris says:

> The righteousness we have is not our own, it comes as God's good gift in Christ. But we will be righteous. Notice that this means more than being pardoned. The pardoned criminal bears no penalty, but he bears a stigma. He is a criminal and he is known as a criminal, albeit an unpunished one. The justified sinner not only bears no penalty; he is righteous. He is not a man with his sins still about him.[8]

Pastorally the full meaning of justification, as pardon and imputed perfection, has proved to be a mighty antidote to despair for the saints. John Bunyan, the author of *Pilgrim's Progress*, was tormented with uncertainty about his standing with God until this doctrine broke in on his soul. He speaks for thousands when he says,

separate them at all, either in speaking or even in thinking. And it is with regard to both these conjointly that Jesus is called 'the Lord our righteousness.'" John Wesley's Sermons, Sermon #20, "The Lord Our Righteousness," preached at the Chapel in West-Street, Seven Dials, on Sunday, November 24, 1765 (see Chapter One, note 15 and Chapter Two, note 3).

John Murray is very helpful here in making the proper use of the language of active and passive obedience. "The term 'passive obedience' does not mean that in anything Christ did was he passive, the involuntary victim of obedience imposed upon him. . . . In his sufferings he was supremely active. . . Neither are we to suppose that we can allocate certain phases or acts of our Lord's life on earth to the active obedience and certain other phases and acts to the passive obedience. The distinction between the active and passive obedience is not a distinction of periods. It is our Lord's whole work of obedience in every phase and period that is described as active and passive, and we must avoid the mistake of thinking that the active obedience applies to the obedience of his life and the passive obedience to the obedience of his final sufferings and death.

"The real use and purpose of the formula is to emphasize the two distinct aspects of our Lord's vicarious obedience. The truth expressed rests upon the recognition that the law of God has both penal sanctions and positive demands. It demands not only the full discharge of its precepts but also the infliction of penalty for all infractions and shortcomings. It is this twofold demand of the law of God which is taken into account when we speak of the active and passive obedience of Christ. Christ as the vicar of his people came under the curse and condemnation due to sin and he also fulfilled the law of God in all its positive requirements. In other words, he took care of the guilt of sin and perfectly fulfilled the demands of righteousness. He perfectly met both the penal and the preceptive requirements of God's law. The passive obedience refers to the former and the active obedience to the latter." John Murray, *Redemption— Accomplished and Applied* (Grand Rapids, MI: William B. Eerdmans, 1955), pp. 20-22.

[7] See Chapter Three, note 26.

[8] Leon Morris, *The Cross in the New Testament* (Grand Rapids, MI: William B. Eerdmans, 1965), p. 247.

One day as I was passing into the field . . . this sentence fell upon my soul. Thy righteousness is in heaven. And methought, withal, I saw with the eyes of my soul Jesus Christ at God's right hand; there, I say, was my righteousness; so that wherever I was, or whatever I was doing, God could not say of me, he wants [=lacks] my righteousness, for that was just [in front of] him. I also saw, moreover, that it was not my good frame of heart that made my righteousness better, nor yet my bad frame that made my righteousness worse, for my righteousness was Jesus Christ himself, "The same yesterday, today, and forever." . . .

Now did my chains fall off my legs indeed. I was loosed from my afflictions and irons; my temptations also fled away; so that from that time those dreadful scriptures of God [e.g., Hebrews 12:16-17] left off to trouble me; now went I also home rejoicing for the grace and love of God.[9]

Alongside the pastoral preciousness of the doctrine of the imputed righteousness of Christ is the great truth that this doctrine bestows on Jesus Christ the fullest honor that he deserves. Not only should he be honored as the one who died to pardon us, and not only should he be honored as the one who sovereignly works faith and obedience in us, but he should also be honored as the one who provided a perfect righteousness for us as the ground of our full acceptance and endorsement by God. I pray that the "newer"[10] ways of understanding justification, which deny the reality of the imputation of divine righteousness to sinners by faith alone, will not flourish, and that the fullest glory of Christ and the fullest pastoral help for souls will not be diminished.

---

[9] John Bunyan, *Grace Abounding to the Chief of Sinners* (Hertfordshire: Evangelical Press, 1978, orig. 1666), pp. 90-91.

[10] Gundry sees himself as part of a larger shift away from the historic doctrine. "It is no accident, then, that in New Testament theologians' recent and current treatments of justification, you would be hard-pressed to find any discussion of an imputation of Christ's righteousness. (I have in mind treatments by Mark Seifrid, Tom Wright, James Dunn, Chris Beker, and John Reumann, among others.) The notion is passé" (I, 9). "Other recognized scholars could easily be added to the list, so many in fact that it would not exaggerate to speak of a developing standard in biblical theological circles" (II, 15).

Desiring God Ministries
720 Thirteenth Avenue South
Minneapolis, Minnesota 55415-1793

Toll free in the USA: 1-888-346-4700
International calls: 001 (612) 373-0651
Fax: (612) 338-4372
mail@desiringGOD.org
www.desiringGOD.org

Desiring God Ministries
United Kingdom
Unit 2B Spencer House
14-22 Spencer Road
Londonderry
Northern Ireland
BT47 6AA
United Kingdom
Tel/fax: 011 (02871) 342 907
dgm.uk@ntlworld.com
www.desiringGOD.org.uk

Scripture Index

Genesis

2:17	97, 100
6:13-14	95
8:16-17	95
15:6	54, 55, 57, 60, 66,116, 118
17:10	95
20:7	95
31:13	95
31:15	57

Exodus

19:12	98, 100

Numbers

18:27	57

Nehemiah

9:33	70

Psalms

32	116-119
32:1-2	57-58

Proverbs

17:15	74

Ecclesiastes

3:1-8	Preface

Isaiah

1:2	31
5:16	70
10:22	70
53:5	118

Jeremiah

23:6	43

Lamentations

1:18	70

Matthew

3:15	43, 113
5:48	123
6:15	123
24:45	108
24:47	108
28:20	32

Luke

12:14	108

John

5:28-29	123
10:18	43

Acts

6:3	108
7:10	108
13:38-39	76
19:10	32
20:27	32

Romans

1—5	77, 93
1—8	13
1—16	26, 32, 43, 49
1:17	66
1:24	72
1:26	72
1:28	72

1:32	95, 100
2:5	107
2:7-8	107
2:15	95
3—4	68, 89
3—5	90
3—6	77
3:20	89
3:20—4:6	65-68
3:21-22	42, 124
3:23	92
3:24-25	41, 115, 124
3:24-26	47, 71-75, 77
3:25-26	67
3:28	58, 59, 64, 77, 89, 107
3:30	58
4	111, 116-119
4:2-6	54-68
4:3	62
4:3-8	116
4:4	116
4:4-6	65
4:5	25, 29, 31, 46, 62, 108, 116
4:6	42, 83, 110, 116, 119, 124
4:6-8	116
4:6-11	119
4:7-8	58
4:9	46, 62, 64, 110
4:9-11	60-61
4:11	42, 58, 62, 64, 83, 116, 119, 124
4:15	97
4:22	46, 62, 64
4:23	64
4:24	46, 116, 119
5	28
5:1	58, 107
5:2	58
5:6-8	25
5:6-11	111
5:9	115, 118
5:10	25, 115
5:12	90-94
5:12-19	81, 90-114
5:12-21	33, 99
5:13-14	94-103

5:15-17	103-106
5:15-19	103
5:17	33, 49, 50, 60, 116
5:18	104, 116
5:18-19	42, 106-110, 124
5:19	82, 104, 111, 116
5:20-21	98
5:21	91, 99, 106
6	50, 101
6—8	78
6:1	49, 77, 99
6:5	50
6:6	50
6:6-7	72, 75-79, 80
6:11	50
6:14	78
6:15	77
6:15-23	72
6:16	101
7	50
7:4	43
7:7-25	72
8	43
8:1	79, 86
8:3	41, 68, 123
8:3-4	79-80
8:4	112
8:13	50, 123
8:23	73, 86
8:33-34	79
9:3	107
9:30	58
9:30—10:4	87-90
10:1-13	66
10:3	87, 89
10:4	14, 87-90, 116, 119
10:6	62
10:10	62

1 Corinthians

1:2	86
1:24	86
1:30	34, 84-87, 89
15:22	102
15:45	103

2 Corinthians

| 4:2 | 70 |

5:19	46, 68, 69
5:21	41, 42, 68-69, 81-83, 84, 86, 89, 90, 116, 118, 119, 123, 124
9:8	89

Galatians

2:11	13
2:16	89
2:17	84, 85, 86
3:2	89
3:5	89
3:6	46, 64
3:10	89, 123
3:13	41, 73, 123
6:8-9	123
6:14	34

Ephesians

1:7	73, 115
2:8-10	89
2:10	86, 89
4:32	28
5:21-25	27

Philippians

1:20	34
2:5-11	24
2:8	119
3:8-9	62, 83-84
3:9	84, 86, 89, 90, 116, 119

Colossians

1:10	89
1:14	73

1 Thessalonians

1:3	89

2 Thessalonians

1:11	89
2:13	123

1 Timothy

5:25	89
6:18	89

2 Timothy

2:21	89
3:17	89

Titus

1:5	108
2:7	89
2:14	89, 122
3:1	89
3:8	89
3:14	89

Hebrews

9:22	115
12:16-17	125

James

2:10	123
2:17	123
2:23	46
4:4	109

1 Peter

2:24	118
3:18	118

2 Peter

1:8	109
3:18	30

1 John

2:17	123
3:14	123

Name Index

Baker, David L., 101

Bancroft, Charitie Lees Smith, 37

Barnett, Paul, 68

Barrett, C. K., 85, 86

Battles, Ford Lewis, 84

Beker, Chris, 45, 125

Belmonte, Kevin Charles, 25

Bromiley, Geoffrey W., 92

Buchanan, James, 46

Buddha, 24

Bunyan, John, 38, 124, 125

Calvin, John, 84

Carson, D. A., 42

Cherry, Edith, 36

Chesterton, G. K. , 30

Confucius, 24

Cook, Steve and Vicki, 37

Cranfield, C. E. B., 67

Das, A. Andrew, 22

Dennis, Lane, 14

Dennison, James T., Jr., 35

DeWitt, John Richard, 73

Dickinson, Emily, 26

Dorman, Ted M., 38

Dunn, James D. G., 42, 45, 125

Edwards, Jonathan, 35, 38, 43, 92, 111

Elwell, Walter A., 90

Eveson, Philip H., 42

Fitzmyer, Joseph, 91

Flavel, John, 86

Fuller, Daniel, 116

Gaffin, Richard, 84

George, Timothy, 24

Giger, George Musgrave, 35

Gill, Thomas, 36

Gundry, Robert, 15, 44-51, 53-125

Hafemann, Scott J., 72

Hagner, Donald A., 42, 82

Harris, Phoebe, 26
Hodge, Charles, 81, 82, 83, 122
Holbrook, Clyde A., 92

Käsemann, Ernst, 92
Kateregga, Badru D., 24
Kendrick, Graham, 37
Kim, Seyoon, 42
Kittel, Gerhard, 109
Koperski, Veronica, 22
Kruse, Colin G., 22

Ladd, George, 81, 82
Luther, Martin, 13

McNeill, John T., 84
Moo, Douglas J., 22, 57, 67, 80, 89, 95
Morris, Leon, 73, 124
Mote, Edward, 36
Muhammad, 24
Murray, John, 46, 64, 92, 95, 96, 107, 114, 124

Nettles, Thomas J., 38
Newton, John, 26

O'Brien, Peter T., 42
Oden, Thomas C., 44, 46
Oepke, Albrecht, 109
Owen, John, 46, 50, 64

Packer, J. I., 89
Perman, Matt, 14
Piper, Barnabas, 63
Piper, Noël, 15
Piper, John, 26, 44, 67, 70
Piper, Talitha, 28, 29
Plass, Ewald M., 13
Pollock, John, 26
Reumann, John, 45, 125
Ridderbos, Herman, 73
Robertson, O. Palmer, 57

Sanders, E. P, 42
Schreiner, Thomas R., 22, 38, 67, 80, 91, 97
Seifrid, Mark A., 42, 45, 125
Shedd, William, 123
Shenk, David W., 24
Simeon, Charles, 26
Sproul, R. C., 42
Steinbach, Carol, 14-15
Steller, Tom, 14
Stuhlmacher, Peter, 42, 72, 73

Taylor, Justin, 14
Thielman, Frank, 22
Turretin, Francis, 35

Ware, Bruce A., 38
Watts, Isaac, 36
Wesley, Charles, 36
Wesley, John, 37, 38, 43, 123, 124
Westerholm, Stephen, 22

White, James R., 42
Whitefield, George, 38, 43
Wilberforce, William, 24, 25,
    26, 34, 44
Woodberry, J. Dudley, 24
Wright, N. T., 42, 86
Wright, Tom, 45, 125

Zinzendorf, Nicolaus L. von,
    37, 41

SUBJECT INDEX

Active and passive obedience,
123-124 n. 6 *See also*
Righteousness of Christ,
Imputation, Forgiveness
Adam
    connection with Christ, 33,
        92-93, 101-106
    sin of imputed to all, 92, 94,
        105
    type of Christ, 101
    universal condemnation and
        corruption from, 33

Biblical theology, and control-
    ling paradigms, 70, 74

Christ
    as second Adam, 103
    both our sin-bearer and righ-
        teousness, 30, 35, 41, 69,
        82-83, 123-124
    deficient views of justifica-
        tion rob him of glory, 34-
        35, 51, 125
    fulfills what Adam failed to
        do, 103

goal of the law, 88
    his supremacy the foundation
        of our joy, 34
    outstrips the destruction of
        Adam, 106
    universal relevance, 33
    worship of, 35-37
Church growth, 22-23, 33
Condemnation, 79
Controversy
    can be for sake of joy, 13-14
    importance of clarity in, 70
        n. 16
Crediting *See* Imputation

Death
    legal consequence of law-
        breaking, 98
    ultimately due to imputation
        of Adam's sin, 91-100,
        102-103
Doctrine
    and September 11, 23-24
    and sermons, 30
    church needs to reclaim, 26
    crucial in church planting, 32

foundation for morality, 25
necessary for a sound church,
  22-23
strengthens families, 30
Wilberforce on, 25

Faith
  borrowed faith, 26
  Gundry's view on relation-
    ship with justification, 47-
    48, 53, 56, 121-122
  not treated as our righteous-
    ness, 54-64
  relation to obedience, 51 n.
    18
  results in good works, 122 n.
    4
Faith imputed as righteousness
  clarifying analogy, 63-64
  meaning of, 60-64, 62 n. 7
Forgiveness *See also*
  Justification
  and redemption, 73
  relation to justification, 29-
    30, 35, 41, 116-119

Glory
  of Christ, 14, 34-35, 39, 51,
    125
  of justification by grace, 93
Grace, 53, 98

Imputation *See also*
  Justification, Righteousness
  of Christ

abandonment of is a massive
  revision of Protestant theology, 35
and biblical terminology of
  "reckoned" and "cred-
  ited," 54-55, 57 n. 4
and bookkeeping metaphor,
  55
antidote to despair, 43, 124-
  125
classic defenses of, 46 n. 9
crediting of Christ's righteousness, not inward
  transformation, 81-83, 93,
  101-102, 110
defending not a rearguard
  action, 48
definition of, 41
glory of, 13, 93
Gundry on, 44-48
importance of, 13-14, 49
in hymns and worship songs,
  36-38
not marginal but central in
  Christian worship, 38
presently impugned and
  imperiled, 13
saves and sweetens mar-
  riages, 27
teaching it to children, 28-30
Wesley affirmed it, 37-38
why relevant to all, 21-39
Infants, and relation to imputation of Adam's sin, 95-100
Infused righteousness

and new view of justification,
48-49
and Roman Catholic view of
justification, 48-49, 49 n.
15
Islam
and ecumenism, 23-24
rejects essentials of
Christianity, 24
same God? 24, n.4

Joy
and supremacy of Christ, 34
from embracing Christ as
righteousness, 33-34, 124-
125
must be truth-based, 23
Justification *See also*
Imputation, Righteousness of
Christ, Righteousness of God
and biblical counseling, 31-
32
and church planting, 33-34
and connection with societal
transformation, 26
and ecumenical dialogues, 42
n. 2
and hope for imperfect parents, 31
and hope for prodigals, 31
and marriage, 27
and raising children, 28
and revival, 43 n. 3
and Roman Catholic posi-
tion, 49 n. 15

and world evangelization,
32-33
apart from works of any
kind, 58, 89, 93, 102, 122-
123
by faith alone, essential for
virtue and holiness, 25, 49-
50
Calvin on relation to union
with Christ, 84 n. 30
ground of sanctification, 50,
77-79, 123
Gundry on, 44-48
importance of, 14, 21-39, 43-
44, 51, 124-125
imputation of righteousness,
not just forgiveness, 29-30,
58, 114-119
"justified from sin," 75-80
Luther on importance of, 13
nature of, 53
not liberation from sin's mastery, 69-80, 104
of ungodly, 57-58
ordinary meaning of, 71, 76,
104, 115
other controversies concerning, 42 n. 2
resources on, 22 n.3
righteousness of Christ basis
of, 105-106
teaching to children, 28-30
universal relevance, 32-33
why not a legal fiction, 89 n.
35

Law
  and Gentiles, 100
  and imputation of sin, 94-
    100
  before Moses, 95
  Christ fulfilled for believers,
    43
  goal of, 88-89
  why Israel failed to attain, 88
Liberation from sin's mastery
  See also Sanctification
  not part of justification, 70-
    80
Love, 34

Missions
  doctrine transfer essential, 32
  justification relevant to all
    people groups, 32-33
New Perspective, resources on,
  42 n. 2

Propitiation, 29, 41-42, 82-83,
  121, 124
Psychology
  doctrine of justification cen-
    tral to wholeness, 31
  psychotherapy, 31

Reckoning See Imputation
Redemption
  and justification, 71-75
  and OT context, 74
  in Romans 3:24, 73-74

legal aspects to, 73 nn. 20,
    21
Righteousness, needed to stand
  before God, 89, 123
Righteousness of Christ See also
  Righteousness of God
  and 1 Corinthians 1:20, 84-
    87
  and Philippians 3:9, 83-84
  and Romans 5:12-19, 90-110
  and Romans 10:4, 87-90
  and 2 Corinthians 5:21, 81-
    83
  basis of believers' eternal life,
    104
  consequences of denying
    imputation of, 112
  consists in his obedience, 41,
    106, 109-110, 112-113
  imputed in justification, 80-
    119
  relation to death of Christ
    and forgiveness, 41-42,
    111 n. 58, 114-119, 123-
    124
  relation to righteousness of
    God, 82-83, 84, 122 n. 2
  single act or whole life?, 112-
    114
Righteousness of God See also
  Righteousness of Christ
  and imputation, 64-69
  and OT context, 74
  and redemption, 74-75

and salvific activity, 70-72, 74

bookkeeping framework vs. covenantal framework, 54-56, 70

relation between attribute and gift, 67 n. 11

Salvation *See* Justification, Sanctification, Redemption, Imputation, Forgiveness

Sanctification

and biblical terminology, 49 nn. 13, 14

and erasure of distinction with justification in newer view, 47, 72, 75

distinction with justification matters, 49-50

justification foundation of, 49-50, 77-80, 123

not part of justification, 49-50, 71

September 11, 23-24

Sin

of Adam imputed to all, 92-93, 100, 102, 105

fighting it as justified sinners, 50

two ways of enslaving, 78

Teaching children

and justification, 28-30

and value of doctrine, 30

Chesterton on, 30

Theology, importance of synthesis in, 90 *See also* Doctrine

Universalism, 107 n. 51

Wesley, John

affirmed imputation, 37-38

resources on his view, 38 n. 15

Works and works of law, 57-58, 89 n. 36